LADS

·LADS·

LOVE POETRY OF THE TRENCHES

MARTIN TAYLOR

DUCKWORTH

First published in paperback in 1998 by
Gerald Duckworth & Company Limited
61 Frith Street
London W1V 5TA

Published in hardback in 1989 by Constable and Company Limited

ISBN 0 7156 2879 8

A catalogue record for this book is available from the British Library.

Printed in Great Britain by
St Edmundsbury Press Limited
Bury St Edmunds, Suffolk

To Ordinary Seamen Ronald Moscrop and Ralph Wray

CONTENTS

YOUTH IN ARMS

THE GREATER LOVE

ENVOI

ACKNOWLEDGEMENTS

I am grateful to the following for permission to use copyright material: to Timothy d'Arch Smith for 'How Rifleman Brown came to Valhalla' in *The Judgement of Valhalla* (1918) by Gilbert Frankau; to The Bodley Head Ltd for 'Trench Poets' and 'War and Peace' from *Collected Poems* (1947) by Edgell Rickword; to Chatto & Windus for "Epilogue to Death of a Hero" from *Death of a Hero* (1928) by Richard Aldington; to Chatto & Windus and the Estate of Robert Nichols for 'The Burial in Flanders', 'By the Wood' and 'Fulfilment' from *Ardours and Endurances* (1917) and for 'Casualty' and 'The Secret' from *Aurelia and Other Poems* (1920); to Rosica Colin Ltd and Catherine Guillaume for 'Concert', 'Epilogue', 'Reserve' and 'Soliloquy 1' in *Collected Poems* (1948) by Richard Aldington; to J. M. Dent & Sons Ltd for 'Lost in France: Jo's Requiem' from *The Leaf Burners, and Other Poems* (1918) by Ernest Rhys; to Faber & Faber Ltd for 'Bitter-fresh' and 'Killed in Action' from *In The Valley of Vision* (1918) and for 'Died of Wounds', 'Mechanic repairing a Motor-cycle', 'The Modern Achilles' and 'The Night you went' from *The Buried Stream* (1941) by Geoffrey Faber, for the extracts from *In Parenthesis* (1937) by David Jones and the extracts from *Hugh Selwyn Mauberley* (1920) by Ezra Pound; to Robert Harben for 'German Boy', 'Joining-up' and 'Over to Flanders' in *Sorrow of War* (1919) by Louis Golding; to Geoffrey Dearmer for 'The Dead Turk' and 'Reality' in *Poems* (1919); to David Higham Associates Ltd for 'Liedholz' and 'My Company' from *Naked Warriors* (1919) by Herbert Read; to Hodder & Stoughton Ltd for 'Dedication', 'The Dead Lover' and 'Missing: Unofficially Reported Killed' in *Dies Heroica* (1918) by J. L. Crommelin Brown; to Macmillan Ltd for 'Elegy' and 'The Halt' in *The Queen of China, and Other Poems* (1919) by Edward Shanks; to Macmillan and Michael Gibson for 'Victory' from *Battle* (1915), 'To Rupert Brooke' from *Friends* (1916), 'Lament' from *Whin* (1917) and 'Mark Anderson' and 'Sentry go' from *Neighbours*

(1920) by Wilfred Gibson; to John Murray (Publishers) Ltd for 'Envoie' from *Poets in Picardy, and Other Poems* (1919) by Edward de Stein, for 'Friendship' and 'Shadow and Light' from *The Temple of Janus* (1917) and 'By the River' from *Mesopotamia* (1919) by James Griffyth Fairfax, and for 'German Prisoners' from *Work-a-Day Warriors* (1917) by Joseph Lee; to Oxford University Press and Robert Haines, Sole Trustee of the Gurney Estate, for 'Farewell', 'First Time In', 'The Mangel-Bury' and 'Strange Hells' from *Collected Poems of Ivor Gurney*; to Peters Fraser & Dunlop Group Ltd for '1916 seen from 1921' and 'The Watchers' in *Poems 1914–1930* (1930) by Edmund Blunden; to George Sassoon for 'Banishment', 'The Death-bed', 'The Dug-out', 'The Effect', 'Enemies', 'Foot Inspection', 'I stood with the Dead', 'In Barracks', 'The Last Meeting', 'Prelude: the Troops', 'Secret Music', 'Sick Leave', 'Suicide in the Trenches' and 'The Triumph' from *The War Poems* (1983) by Siegfried Sassoon; to Unwin Hyman Ltd for 'News' from *Years of Peace* (1925) by Godfrey Elton, and for 'To my Mate' from *Any Soldier to his Son* (1919) and 'Two years after' from *A Ballad of Four Brothers* (1921) by George Willis; to A. P. Watt Ltd for 'Not Dead' and 'Two Fusiliers' from *Fairies and Fusiliers* (1917) by Robert Graves, and for 'The Bathe' from *Half-Hours at Helles* (1916) and 'The German Graves' from *The Bomber Gypsy* (1918) by A. P. Herbert; to Faber & Faber Ltd for the extract from 'The Waste Land', from *Collected Poems 1909–1962* by T. S. Eliot; and to Sidgwick and Jackson Ltd for 'Return' from *A Muse at Sea* (1919) by E. Hilton Young.

The illustrations are by William Kermode and are taken from *A Patriot's Progress* (London: Geoffrey Bles, 1930) by Henry Williamson. The lines from 'Keep the home fires burning' by L. G. Ford are reproduced by permission of Chappell Music Ltd, London.

I would like to thank the following people for their advice and encouragement; Robin Baird-Smith, Terry Charman, Peter Parker, Michael Slater, Peter Twist and David Goudge.

M.T.
1989

INTRODUCTION

THE characteristics of First World War poetry are thrown into obvious relief by a comparison with the poetry of the Second World War. Of the many differences, a subject that requires a book in itself, the most obvious is the difference in emotional tone. As Paul Fussell observes in his masterly chapter 'Soldier Boys' in *The Great War and Modern Memory*: 'No one turning from the poetry of the Second World War to that of the First can fail to notice there the unique physical tenderness, the readiness to admire openly the bodily beauty of young men, the unapologetic recognition that men may be in love with each other.'[1] The reality of this emotion is a fact accepted by most military historians, as John Ellis indicates in *Eye-deep in Hell: the Western Front 1914–1918*: 'There was also love for one's comrades. The word is not used carelessly. Nothing else can describe the devotion and selflessness that characterized the relationship of men within the same platoon or company.'[2] The purpose of this anthology is to introduce a wider selection of poets and poetry than those used by Fussell, and to suggest some further ideas on this remarkable phenomenon.

Bracketed by the Criminal Law Amendment Act of 1885 and the post-war writings of Freud, Adler, Jung and Krafft-Ebing, the First World War saw the swansong of the romantic friendships that had distinguished the Victorian period. W. T. Stead, who was largely responsible for the 1885 Act but who abhorred the attendant Labouchère Amendment which made all homosexual acts illegal, wrote to Edward Carpenter; 'A few more cases like Oscar Wilde's and we should find the freedom of comradeship now possible to men seriously impaired to the detriment of the race.'[3] If the trial of Wilde brought the irrefutable existence of homosexuality to the attention of the late-Victorian public, the psychologists of the early twentieth century made a new generation aware of the ambivalent impulses underlying male comradeship. But for the duration of the First World War, and in the hearts of those that survived, romantic friendships flourished.

Fussell eschews the term 'romantic friendship' for the more expressive 'homo-eroticism', which he qualifies as 'a sublimated (i.e. "chaste") form of temporary homosexuality . . . like the "idealistic", passionate but non-physical "crushes" which most . . . officers had experienced at public school.'[4] Much of the best of First World War poetry is characterized by a strong homo-erotic element, but it is a consideration that requires very careful treatment if its complexities are to be fully understood. Sentiments that appear to the modern reader to be overtly homosexual were written and published, without embarrassment or censure, in an age that could still remember the fall of Wilde and the scandal of Cleveland Street. And expressions of love for one's comrades did not only appear in the elevated medium of verse, but also in the more prosaic form of letters and personal diaries. Most reflections on the First World War experience contain some anecdote revealing an affection between fighting-men that went beyond the bounds of ordinary comradeship. The pervasiveness of the emotion is matched only by its unselfconsciousness. This qualification is not intended to diminish the homo-erotic element of First World War literature, but simply to warn readers against adopting too unguarded an approach. Indeed, it needs to be stressed that too much literary obfuscation of the theme has already taken place.

In his introduction to *Siegfried Sassoon Diaries 1915–1918*, Rupert Hart-Davies remarks that '[Sassoon's] first three prose works . . . were autobiography disguised as fiction, by changing the names of everyone he met . . . and by making no reference to his being a poet. A close comparison of these books with his diaries shows they are faithful records of his experiences, based on his contemporary descriptions, occasionally heightened but never distorted.'[5] This statement is true, but not quite accurate, as the diaries themselves reveal. Sassoon, for obvious reasons, made no published reference to his homosexuality. Too scrupulous a man to lie, he chose instead to negotiate the issue by recasting fact as fiction, with a central character based on himself. A comparison of the following passages from *Sherston's Progress* and the *Diaries* reveal exactly what was omitted in the process.

> When I rode into the transport lines this afternoon I saw young Stonethwaite drudging at cleaning a limber, supervised by a military policeman.
>
> He has still got ten days to do, of his 28 days 'Field Punishment No. 2' for coming drunk on parade at Marseilles. I gave him a cheery nod and a grin, and he smiled back at me as he stood there in his grimy slacks and blue jersey. I hadn't spoken to him since I 'talked to him like a father' when he was awaiting his court martial. He was in the other Company I was with for a time in Palestine, and I took an interest in him, partly because he'd served with our First Battalion in France, and partly because of the noticeably nice look in his face. (He was the sort of chap no one could help liking.) . . . So I went into the shed at Domvast where he was shut up and talked to him about making a fresh start and so on. And I suppose he felt grateful to me, standing there with his white face and his eyes full of tears. Seeing him there this afternoon I felt glad I'd been kind to him.[6]

> Then I saw [Jim Linthwaite], digging away at road-mending, and he'd got a rotten pair of boots, which were an excuse for conversation, and I've loved him ever since (it is just as well he's not in my present Company). And when he got into trouble I longed to be kind to him. And I talked to him about 'making a fresh start and not doing anything silly again', while he stood in front of me with his white face, and eyes full of tears. I suppose I'd have done the same for any man in the Company who had a good character. But there was a great deal of sex floating about in this particular effort. No doubt he dreams about 'saving my life'. I wish I could save his.[7]

This must necessarily alter our understanding of Sassoon, for it locates the emotional impulse behind his work. Edna St Vincent Millay, who had attended one of Sassoon's poetry readings in America after the war, remarked: 'I wonder whether he would have cared so much if it were a thousand virgins who had been slaughtered.'[8] And we can, perhaps unfairly, expand upon this question by asking whether he would have been so moved had not the dead included a large proportion of beautiful young men. Throughout the *Diaries* Sassoon enthuses about the young men who catch his eye, but he was less affected when confronted by soldiers neither so attractive nor so impressionable. The Whelan Brothers, the famous music-hall comedians whom he describes rehearsing for a concert, bring out a less gallant aspect of his character:

> A big man was doing a bit of a gag before stepping back two paces to start his song. 'Give 'em a bit of Fred Emney' shouts someone, then a little man jumps into the light, and does some posturing, chin out, with his curved Hebrew beak coming down to his thin-lipped mouth. Another little Jew whispered to me . . . 'That's Sid Whelan – the other's his brother Albert' – evidently expected me to be thrilled. Probably well known London comedians.[9]

This is not meant to diminish Sassoon, but rather to emphasize that his response to the war had a more particular source than a generalized, universal love of humanity. His compassion for all soldiers sprang from his vision of their individual beauty: 'I watch the men lying about on the decks in the sunlight . . . I like to see them leaning against each other with their arms round one another – it is pathetic and beautiful and human.'[10] Ironically, Sassoon as Sherston, shorn of his homosexuality, is a more representative figure than the real Sassoon. Many men experienced relationships that although sexually innocent, were deeper and more emotional than simple camaraderie, or even marriage. And it is one of the tragedies of the First World War that the flowering of such cryptic and delicate emotions should have been occasioned by an operation involving so much human wastage. As Arthur Graeme West observed:

> How rare life is!
> On earth, the love and fellowship of men,
> Men sternly banded: banded for what end?
> Banded to maim and kill their fellow men.[11]

When asked by Eleanor Farjeon, 'Do you know what you are fighting for?', Edward Thomas in response bent down, picked up a handful of soil and, rubbing it between his fingers, replied, 'Literally, for this.'[12]

Wilfred Owen's 'handful of soil' was 'a Harrow boy, of superb intellect and refinement; intellect because he hates war more than Germans; refinement because of the way he spoke of my Going, and of the Sun, and of the Sea there; and the way he spoke of Everything. In fact, the way he spoke –'; and he described the boy to his mother as 'the best piece of the Nation left in England'.[13] Owen came to fight for the possibilities of life that his war experiences had revealed to him, and many soldiers found themselves fighting for something at the end of the war that they had not considered at its outset. King and Country had become less important than 'the boy at [one's] side'.[14] But in the first three years of the war the three million men that enlisted did so at the call of patriotism, and for those who demonstrated reluctance, conscription, which had been unthinkable in pre-war Britain, was introduced in 1916. Many men of literary sensitivity, like Sassoon and Owen, who would never have ordinarily considered a military career, suddenly found themselves with little preparation thrown into the role of fighting-men, and the poems in the first section of this anthology, THE CALL, are intended to reveal something of the excitement and apprehension they felt.

The most famous of the early recruits was Rupert Brooke, whose early death became for some a symbol of the waste of war, and for others a testament to heroic sacrifice. Brooke's volume of poetry *1914: and Other Poems* was one of the most popular of the period, running to twenty-five impressions by the end of the war, and was also the first of many such volumes to celebrate a 'fallen hero'. A vaguely necrophiliac air pervades this aspect of First World War poetry, for death ensured publication and popularity. Arthur Graeme West, who was killed in action in April 1917 and whose *Diary of a Dead Officer*, published in 1918, is one of the most uncharacteristic memorial volumes, was moved to complain:

> God! How I hate you, you cheerful young men,
> Whose pious poetry blossoms on your graves
> As soon as you are in them, nurtured up
> By the salt of your corruption, and the tears
> Of mothers, local vicars, college deans,
> And flanked by prefaces and photographs

From all your minor poet friends—the fools—
Who paint their sentimental elegies
Where sure, no angel treads; and living, share
The dead's brief immortality.[15]

The public appetite for such volumes was largely attributable to a civilian guilt at not fighting; but out of this there developed a less attractive taste for accounts of young men cut down in their prime. Sentimental notions of sacrifice and martyrdom, often encouraged by the poets themselves who died with 'the truth untold' on their lips rather than on paper, rationalized the slaughter of millions. This, however, was little comfort to the men at the front, where the ugliness of life and death in the trenches precluded any such exalted perceptions. Sassoon's criticism of women at home, 'O their gluttonous eyes: I think they love war, for all their lamenting over the sons and lovers', would have been better applied to the nation's attitude to her dead soldiers, an idea he was to focus on in 'Suicide in the trenches'.[16]

Brooke's popularity was due as much to his apposite poems as to his obvious good looks, the former immortalized by his early death in April 1915, and the latter by the famous bare-shouldered photograph by Sherrill Schell. That such an androgynous image, known to Brooke's friends as 'your favourite actress', should have become one of the most famous icons of the First World War reveals a public taste for homo-eroticism, albeit spiritualized, that helps to account for the enormous popularity of soldier-poet verse. 'Sonnet to Rupert Brooke', by the Australian soldier-poet Peter Austen, is one of the more extravagantly homo-erotic tributes to the dead poet, and demonstrates how far-reaching his reputation was:

Oh Lovely Lover! No, thou art not fled!
    From thy red mouth blow poppies glowingly!
And the wild hyacinth above thy head,
    Sprang from the tender, dreaming eyes of thee!

Hark! From that thicket, sounds a thrilling thrush;
    It is thy boy's voice raised aloft to bless—
All quiv'ring thro' the morning's dewy hush—
    The rose's dear, unthrifty loveliness.

So, when the moist sea-wind with wistful croon,
  Touches my happy mouth caressingly,
I shall go singing, singing 'neath the moon—
  Knowing, somewhere, it kissed the eyes of thee!
Oh Lovely Lover! Beauty cannot die
  Thus doest thou live forever to our eye![17]

Before the war Brooke had been the object of much homosexual interest at public school and among the Cambridge Apostles, and it is thought that one of his reasons for enlisting was to evade his own feelings of sexual confusion. That Brooke was finally incarcerated by the very aura he had tried to escape is largely the responsibility of his devoted mentor Edward Marsh, whose sanitized memoir of Brooke, published with the *Collected Poems* of 1918, fully endorsed the legend. Significantly, Edward Marsh and Harold Monro of the Poetry Bookshop, who had published Brooke's poems in the first edition of *Georgian Poetry*, were responsible for mediating much of the soldier-poet verse to the public.

Brooke died without experiencing the trench warfare that was to become the central experience for the soldiers of the First World War. His one military engagement, the Royal Naval Division expedition to Antwerp in October 1914, was a dying echo of another more traditional type of war. The stalemate that developed on the Western Front, with two enormous armies seemingly capable only of effective defence, ushered in a modern warfare of gas and machine-guns, large casualties and little movement. Most military commanders were slow to recognize that the character of warfare had radically changed, and were thus unable to devise any effective strategic response. Inevitably, many lives were lost in the war of attrition waged on the Western Front to diminish the German forces as a necessary prelude to victory; but many lives were also needlessly thrown away, and this left an indelible impression on the men at the front.

Life in the trenches was an unprecedented experience for both regular and new army soldiers, and the poems in the section SOMEWHERE IN FRANCE reflect the impact of this new experience. In the horrific conditions of the front line, where the threat of death and disfigurement was omnipresent, there developed a mutual feeling of dependence and compassion between soldiers, a relationship that was both general and particular, as well as cutting through barriers of rank. Although armies were vast impersonal organizations, in practice men found themselves bound in small units which developed an intense group loyalty. Frederic Manning wrote movingly in *The Middle Parts of Fortune*:

> These apparently rude and brutal natures comforted, encouraged and reconciled each other to fate, with a tenderness and tact which was far more moving than anything in life. They had nothing; not even their own bodies, which had become mere implements of warfare. They turned from the wreckage and misery of life to an empty heaven, and from an empty heaven to the silence of their own hearts. They had been brought to the last extremity of hope, and yet they put their hands on each others' shoulders and said with a passionate conviction that it would be all right, though they had faith in nothing, but in themselves and in each other.[18]

Within the larger group loyalty there further developed particular friendships which, forged in the circumstances of war, had no parallel in civilian life. One English soldier wrote: 'The love that grows quickly and perhaps artificially when men are together up against life and death has a peculiar quality. Death that cuts it off does not touch the emotions at all, but works right into the soul of you.'[19] Henry Williamson wrote graphically, but eloquently, of the death of a comrade:

> Blood ran down from a hole in his right temple. The back of his head was open like an egg, hairy with thick blood and broken-sploshed grey brains. He snored and gurgled and twitched. Blood trickled from his ears and mouth; he kicked, blew blood bubbles from his nostrils. They heaved him over the parados when he died.[20]

The effect of the death of a soldier on his best friend could be devastating. In *The Middle Parts of Fortune* Bourne goes berserk when his friend Martlow is killed, and shoots three Germans attempting to surrender. The poems in the section KILLED IN ACTION further testify to the overwhelming feeling of shock at the death of a comrade.

Isolated from ordinary life, most soldiers inevitably came to invest all their care and affection in their comrades, usually with a total disregard for the wider issues of the war, other than its conclusion. As C. E. Montague observed in *Disenchantment*: 'all that mattered to [the soldier] was the one little boatload of castaways with whom he was marooned on a desert island and making shift to keep off the weather and any sudden attack of wild beasts.'[21] But the mutual respect, trust and affection that constituted comradeship had to be earned. 'Constantly jammed up against each other,' wrote Montague, 'every man in each of these isolated knots of adventurers came to be seen by the rest for what he was worth, with the drastic clearness of open-eyed husbands and wives of long standing.'[22] For those who were found worthy there resulted, as Herbert Read wrote to a friend in June 1917, 'a wonderful comradeship which I think would overcome any horror or hardship. It is this comradeship which alone makes the Army bearable to me.'[23]

The most significant of the relationships made at the front was that between officers and their men. Although the distinction between officers and men was always clearly marked and carefully maintained, within these boundaries there developed relationships of great intensity, to which poems like Herbert Read's 'My Company' and E. A. Mackintosh's 'In memoriam' eloquently testify. For many middle- and upper-class officers, often plucked straight from public school or some equally cloistered social existence, the men were a revelation. Officers' memoirs and letters repeatedly pay tribute to the stoicism and endurance, often in the very worst of circumstances, of the soldiers under their command. Lieutenant-Colonel Richard Fielding wrote to his wife:

> I can never express in writing what I feel about the men in the trenches; and nobody who has not seen them can ever understand ... You may ask any one of them, any moment of the day or night, 'Are you cold?' or 'Are you wet?' – and you will get but one answer ... always with a smile – 'Not too cold, sir' or 'Not too wet, sir'. It makes me feel sick.[24]

The perspective from the other side of the relationship is less well documented: ordinary soldiers tended not to be so articulate on paper. Montague records that: 'Officers . . . were sorted out by the minds of the men into themes for contemptous silence, objects of love that doeth and beareth all things, and cases of Not Proven Yet.'[25] For those who were prepared to share the same danger as their men, the devotion they received was absolute. H. L. Simpson wrote: 'He sings dirty songs and swears, and is altogether a sensual drunken beast at times; but get to know him, start by loving him, and believe in him through thick and thin, and you will not go unrewarded.'[26] That soldiers rose in waves to go over the top, with only the promise of death, on occasions like 1 July 1916, is a testament to the relationship that developed between officers and their men. Breaking through barriers of rank, class and military protocol, Lance-Corporal A. Laird wrote to the widow of Brigadier-General Frank Maxwell:

> He sat for about two minutes, then he got up again to show what he was saying to the captain, and was just opening his mouth when he got shot. I caught him as he was falling and jumped into a shell hole with him. I held his head against my breast till it was all over. Madam, I cried till my heart was liking to burst.[27]

The relationship between men of equal rank was even more intense, because it developed without restrictions. One of the most powerful portraits of camaraderie between ordinary soldiers is in *The Middle Parts of Fortune*. Although the men are often coarse and abusive, Manning shows that they have a concern for each other that rises 'to an intensity of feeling which friendship never touches'.[28] This is most apparent in Pritchard's description of the death of his friend Swale, where his almost laconic attitude fully indicates the absolute depth of his grief:

> '. . . both 'is legs 'ad been blown off, pore bugger; an' 'e were dyin' so quick you could see it. But 'e tried to stand up on 'is feet. "'elp me up," 'e says, "'elp me up." – "You lie still, chum," I sez to 'im, "you'll be all right presently." An' 'e jes gives me one look, like 'e were puzzled, an' 'e died.'

. . .

> 'Well, anyway,' said Martlow, desperately comforting; ''e could'nt 'ave felt much, could 'e, if 'e said that?' 'I don't know what 'e felt,' said Pritchard, with slowly filling bitterness. 'I know what I felt.'[29]

For many officers the war provided an arena for the continuation of the all-male environment of public school and Oxbridge, and J. B. Priestley, whose education had been grammar school and journalism, recalled: 'I never hailed with relief, as men in the opposing class did, a wholly masculine way of life uncomplicated by woman.'[30] Public-school boys were conditioned by their education to welcome both the institutional and the emotional conditions of war. With the growth of the Empire and the attendant imperialist ideology, English culture, and public schools in particular, became increasingly militaristic; and the establishment of organizations like the Officers' Training Corps was paralleled by an ethos that sentimentalized war as a sport and life as a game, a fallacy that survived into the First World War in poems like 'The call' by R. E. Vernède:

> Lad, with the merry smile and the eyes
> Quick as a hawk's and clear as the day,
> You, who have counted the game the prize,
> Here is the game of games to play,
> Never a goal—the captains say—
> Matches the one that's needed now:
> Put the old blazer and cap away—
> England's colours await your brow.[31]

The emotional response was equally well anticipated. At a period when the sexes were almost totally segregated, it was possible for a boy to have no experience of women beyond members of his own family. A young man going to the front straight from university might be in the same emotional state as a boy straight out of public school, and it was inevitable that the romantic friendships of their childhood and puberty, which had provided mutual reassurances against fear and loneliness, should re-create themselves in the more extreme circumstances of war. Significantly, R. C. Sherriff's *Journey's End* features both a public-school relationship, between Stanhope and Raleigh, and one forged in the trenches, between Stanhope and Osborne.

Neither should we underestimate the erotic quality of these romantic friendships. Although the public-school novels of the pre-war period, *Julian Home*, *Tim*, *The Hill*, *Gerald Eversley's Friendship* and *David Blaize*, are insistent upon the purity of the relationships they feature, the frequent abjurations against 'beastliness' indicate how widespread the 'problem' was.[32] This, no doubt, accounts for H. C. Duffin's assertion in his introduction to H. L. Simpson's posthumous book of war poems, *Moods and Tenses*, that although Simpson had a passion for 'friendships', we are still to 'conceive one, who up to the very end, was everything we mean by healthy boyhood.'[33] No such prevarication, however, from Robert Graves, who wrote with characteristic asperity in the 1929 edition of *Goodbye to All That*:

> In English preparatory and public schools romance is necessarily homosexual. The opposite sex is despised and hated, treated as something obscene. Many boys never recover from this perversion. I only recovered by a shock at the age of twenty-one. For every one born homosexual there are at least ten permanent homosexuals made by the public-school system. And nine of these ten are as honourably chaste and sentimental as I was.[34]

With rather more tenderness than Graves, Sassoon stresses the emotional link between school and the army, when he reflects upon the death of David Thomas, beloved of both Graves and Sassoon:

> But they came afterwards and told me that my little Tommy had been hit by a stray bullet and died last night. When I last saw him, two nights ago, he had his notebook in his hand, reading my last poem. And I said goodnight to him, in the moonlit trenches. Had I but known! – the old human-weak cry. Now he comes back to me in memories, like an angel, with the light in his yellow hair, and I think of him at Cambridge last August when we lived together four weeks in Pembroke College in rooms where the previous occupant's name, Paradise, was written above the door.[35]

Eric Hiscock, writing in 1976 and perhaps heavily affected by hindsight, is rather more revealing than either Graves or Sassoon. Recalling his close friendship with two soldiers, Brook and Jackson, he decides: 'we were close-knit, but as heterosexual as it was possible to be in such a man-made, man-populated community as the 29th Royal Fusiliers, in Flanders. Obviously, we masturbated (but not each other), and the affection that existed between us was confined to the sharing of duties, the opening of parcels from home, and the appreciation of what Rupert Brooke called the "rough male kiss of blankets".'[36] Hiscock also remembers an incident when he was assaulted by another soldier: 'I awoke from an uneasy sleep to find him pressed up close to me and that his hand was undoing my fly-buttons . . . I groaned inwardly. Another bugger'; and the unpleasant and unprepossessing Lieutenant Clark who persecuted Hiscock and coveted his friend Brook: '. . . he was especially drawn to Brook whose golden hair, laughing face, and tall slim body might have stirred any trench-bound male even more disciplined sexually than Clark.'[37] But the central relationship between Hiscock and Brook is as chaste as anything in classic First World War literature:

> [Brook] took my hand in his, and looked into my eyes. There was no laughing light in his as he said softly: 'Love's a wonderful thing. I think we've experienced it at times, haven't we?' . . . There was nothing embarrassing in what he was saying. I had known before we were in love with each other and such a feeling left us both immune from the need or urge for sex. What else is it but love that makes one wonder where someone is, and how he is, and when he will appear at one's side after waking in the morning.[38]

The sexual innocence of these relationships was an important factor. Given the physical conditions of the front line, the filth, the lice and the lack of privacy, and the probable sexual orientation of most soldiers, it is unlikely that any sexual contact was possible or even desirable. The tawdriness of the only vestiges of active heterosexuality in the war zone, the prostitutes in the regulation brothels, could only have encouraged the sanctification of male camaraderie; and the very fact that these emotional relationships had no integral sexual outlet, or even a satisfactory parallel one, only served further to intensify them.

There are, unsurprisingly, very few published references to active homosexuality at the front. Raymond Asquith in a letter to Lady Diana Manners in September 1916 wrote: 'I had two terribly strenuous days – 10 hours each before a court martial defending a fellow officer upon 5 charges of "homosexualism" – unsuccessfully. It was terribly tiring but not entirely unenjoyable as it was easy to make fools of most of the witnesses (though not unfortunately as to the facts to which they testified).'[39] This would appear to have been a relatively rare case, and the experience of J. R. Ackerley, a reliable and not disinterested witness, would seem to have been the more common one: 'During the war I never met a recognizable or self-confessed adult homosexual . . . ; the army with its male relationships was simply an extension of my public school.'[40] Richard Aldington in his 'Prologue' to *Death of a Hero* is rather more emphatic on this point:

> Friendships between soldiers during the war were a real and beautiful and unique relationship which has now entirely vanished, at least from Western Europe. Let me at once disabuse the eager-eyed Sodomites among my readers by stating emphatically once and for all that there was nothing sodomitical in these friendships. I have lived and slept for months, indeed years, with 'the troops', and had several such companionships. But no vaguest proposal was ever made to me; I never saw any sign of sodomy, and never heard anything to make me suppose it existed. However, I was with the fighting troops. I can't answer for what went on behind the lines.
>
> No, no. There was no sodomy about it. It was just a human relationship, a comradeship, an undemonstrative exchange of sympathies between ordinary men racked to extremity under a great common strain in a great common danger.[41]

Aldington's black-and-white denial is tempered by the grey of Ackerley's observation that: 'My personal runners and servants were usually chosen for their looks; indeed this tendency in war to have the prettiest soldiers about one was observable in many other officers'.[42] Graves supplies the obverse of this situation in his play *But it Still Goes On*, where a character remarks: 'Do you know how a platoon of men will absolutely worship a good-looking gallant young officer? . . . Of course, they don't realize exactly what's happening, neither does he; but it's a very, very strong romantic link . . . My men adored me and were showing off all the time before the other companies.'[43] Writing many years later, C. E. Carrington reiterated Aldington's statement but also wondered if 'the soldier's life satisfied hidden desires at a deep level of the mind. Some emotional need was met by the necessity to exert the whole of one's nervous strength in generous rivalry with one's friends.'[44] This all admits to a greater complexity of feeling than Aldington allows.

At the time of writing *Death of a Hero* (1929), the concept of the romantic friendship was no longer tenable, and Aldington was attempting a retrospective defence of a type of relationship that had since come under close scrutiny: even at a literary level, with D. H. Lawrence's portraits of Gerald Crich and Rupert Birkin in *Women in Love* (1920) and Aaron Sissons and Rawdon Lily in *Aaron's Rod* (1922). The work of the post-war psychologists had made it difficult to distinguish the threshold between friendship and homosexuality, maintaining that when the erotic forces of physical attraction motivated a relationship between men, it could then be termed homosexual rather than platonic. Many relationships were, and are, thus motivated, often quite unconsciously, but the suggestion of such a motivation was highly offensive to many men of Aldington's generation.

Aldington, however, is neither honest nor perceptive enough to realize that the constant contemplation of destruction and death in the trenches created an atmosphere where physical wholeness and emotional tenderness were things to be cherished. And Aldington's insistence on the purity of the relationships he encountered should not blind us to the fact that the philosophy of platonic love has frequently been used to describe relationships that only by evasion or restraint have excluded physical expression. An interesting illustration of this idea can be found in J. R. Ackerley's play *The Prisoners of War*, which contains two homo-erotic relationships: between Conrad and Grayle, and Tetford and Rickman. Conrad's mental breakdown is partly occasioned by his attempts to turn his relationship from a homo-erotic to a homosexual one, and he admits at one point to 'being attracted to others in a way that terrifies me'.[45] Tetford, on the other hand, is prepared to accept the limitations of his relationship, and opts for a more straightforward camaraderie: 'We'd pull along together all right, I guess – and you need me to keep a hold on you.'[46]

But this is a complex, and still unresolved, issue, and one of which the writers of the time were conscious. David Jones offered a rationalization of the problem with his portrayal of two distinct relationships in *In Parenthesis*, published in 1937: between the 'lovers from Ebury Bridge, Bates and Coldpepper that men called the lily-white boys' and 'Dynamite Davies the old 'un and Diamond Phelps his batty'; but the intensity of both relationships is comparable, even though the connection between the former pair is a sexual one.

One contemporary method of resolving any confusions aroused by the phenomenon of camaraderie was to describe it in terms of the Greek ideal of male love, as represented by Achilles and Patroclus. Patrick Shaw-Stewart's only war poem, written after hearing of the death of his friend Edward Horner, invokes the famous pair and draws obvious parallels with the circumstances of their deaths:

I saw a man this morning
  Who did not want to die:
I asked and cannot answer,
  If otherwise wish I.

. . .

Achilles came to Troyland
  And I to Chersonese:
He turned from wrath to battle,
  And I from three days' peace.[47]

This, however, begged more questions than it answered. Most officers, being public-school men, would have received a classical education, and their letters, diaries and poems are full of classical allusions and references. Although not encouraged to read the less respectable passages from the classics, most would have done so, and a close examination of Homer and Aeschylus would have revealed that Achilles and Patroclus were not only comrades but also lovers. In E. M. Forster's

Maurice, written in 1913, the hero and his friend Clive reach an understanding of each other by reference to Plato's *Symposium*; and barely a year later, public-school officers would have found themselves serving in a land littered with poppies, not at that stage recognized as the symbol of death, but as one of the flowers with which Corydon courts Alexis in Virgil's *Second Eclogue.* Of particular poignance to sentimentally inclined officers in the trenches was the fact that Corydon's love for Alexis was never consummated, something that would not have influenced them as schoolboys. Significantly, Edward Carpenter's 'anthology of friendship' *Iolaus* (known in the book trade as 'the Bugger's Bible') was republished in 1915, and contained all the appropriate passages from the classics, including Homer, Aeschylus, Virgil and Plutarch on the Theban Band.

This last reference had a special significance, for as Robert Graves has pointed out, the Theban Band of comrades were 'a regiment of mature soldiers, each paired with a younger homosexual companion, who fought to the death in defence of the country and in honour of their love bond'; and in Ackerley's *The Prisoners of War*, Adelby communicates his sympathy for Conrad by referring to Plutarch's *Lives* and the Theban Band.[48] More suitable as a model for a relationship between men that was chaste but passionate was that of David and Jonathan, implied in such poems as Harold Monro's 'Youth in arms' sequence. Similarly, any over-indulgence in the contemplation of individual soldiers could be sanitized by invoking the figure of Christ.

The tradition of the Theban Band was obviously not a feature of the British Army, although something of its spirit did emerge on the Western Front. There was more of the original element in the Arab forces led by T. E. Lawrence. In *Seven Pillars of Wisdom* the ideal is enacted by Farraj and Daud, and Lawrence obviously tried to live something of the ideal with Dahoum, although the relationship was probably platonic – that is, homo-erotic rather than homosexual. Lawrence considered the love of Farraj and Daud to be worthier than heterosexual love, and he wrote that 'friends quivering together in the yielding sand with intimate hot limbs in supreme embrace, found there hidden in the darkness a sensual co-efficient of the mental passion which was welding our souls and spirits in one flaming effort.'[49] This positing of the superior power of a sexual and political unity is very much in the tradition of the Theban Band; and it also serves to remind us that one of Lawrence's reasons for his involvement in the Arab Revolt was 'because I liked a particular Arab very much', namely Dahoum or Sheik Ahmed, to whom the poem 'To S.A.', which prefaces *Seven Pillars of Wisdom*, is dedicated.[50]

No one on the Western Front was ever forced to face the ultimate reality of his feelings in the way that Lawrence was, with his traumatic torture and homosexual rape by the Turks at Deraa in 1917. He recorded his recollection of 'smiling idly' at the corporal in charge of the assault, at the very climax of his agony, 'for a delicious warmth, probably sexual, was swelling through me'.[51] Having been forced to accept the terrifying realization that part of him had wanted to be sodomized, Lawrence could no longer hide behind the illusion of simple camaraderie, and he was propelled on a course of self-punishment and self-abasement. In 1923 Lawrence persuaded a young Scotsman, John Bruce, with whom he was serving in the Tank Corps, to flog him at regular intervals over a period of eleven years, sometimes on the anniversary of the incident at Deraa. This ritualistic flagellation revived his sexual pleasure as well as his sexual guilt, but without resolving either. The situation continued until Lawrence's death in 1935.

Lawrence's is an extreme case, but something similar can be detected in Robert Graves's reaction to the news that his 'wholesome and clean-living' friend 'Peter' ('Dick' in *Goodbye to All That*, and later identified as G. H. Johnstone) had been arrested in 1917 for making a homosexual advance to a soldier:

> The news was nearly the end of me. I decided that Dick had been driven out of his mind by the war. There was madness in his family, I knew; he had once shown me a letter from his grandfather scrawled in circles all over the page. It would be easy to think of him as dead.[52]

Graves' early poetry shows a wilful *naïveté* and a parallel fear of sex, for which he found an outlet in his sentimental attachment to his school-friend. One poem, 'Oh, and oh!', published in *Over the Brazier* in 1917 and written during training in Lancaster, clearly reveals this sexual unease in the comparison between the 'loathsome love' of 'loutish he and sluttish she' and the purity of his feelings for 'Peter'.[53] His revulsion at the sexual pollution of their relationship, perhaps because the sexual possibilities of the relationship were suddenly revealed, left Graves with a homophobia that led him to dismiss Owen as 'a passive homosexual weakling', and later to embrace a religiose heterosexuality that found its apotheosis in the White Goddess system and the subjugation of all things male to the power of the female.[54] Graves never forgave 'Peter' for allowing reality to intrude on their relationship and never again communicated with him, even refusing a legacy of books when 'Peter' died in 1949.

The confusion of sentiments that are magnified in the cases of Lawrence and Graves were, no doubt, common to most soldiers. Something of this confusion informs James S. Yates' confession that: 'I felt myself ever and again strangely comforted by the pure and sweet presence of a young lad of those in my charge; who offered me his friendship, moved by some unknown imaginary act of mine.'[55] Many found their new relationships outside any previous experience, and therefore difficult to define. Herbert Read, whose poems are some of the most intense, wrote: 'We did not call it love; we did not acknowledge its existence; it was sacramental and therefore secret.'[56] Not so secret, however, that it was not written about. It was inevitable that these unanticipated feelings should seek some expression, for relief as well as control, and in the difficult conditions of the front line poetry flourished as the most practicable form of expression. As Ivor Gurney was to say in 'Farewell':

> There was not one of all that battalion
> Loved his comrades as well as I – but kept shy.
> Or said in verse, what his voice would not rehearse.

Given the subject matter and the amateur status of most poets, the most obvious literary model was the poetry previously reserved to express romantic love between men and women. This had the effect of making some poems seem less ambiguous than intended. Robert Nichols, the hysterically heterosexual author of *Sonnets to Aurelia* addressed to Nancy Cunard, was, on the strength of his first volume, *Ardours and Endurances*, listed in the anonymous Uranian bibliography *Catalogue of*

Selected Books from the Library of a Student of Boyhood, Youth, and Comradeship of 1924. But this perception of Nichols' work was not the common one, for Nichols was a critically acclaimed figure and his verse attracted no adverse comments. Indeed, he made a successful career out of reciting his torrid poems to the literary salons of London. Nichols' popularity indicates that intense relationships between men had not yet come under suspicion, and especially not those contracted while fighting for King and Country.

The licence and encouragement extended to poets like Nichols prompted others to seize the opportunity to proclaim publicly their unambiguous love for other men. Sassoon's poem to David Thomas, 'The last meeting', not only would not have been written, but also would not have been openly published, without the war; his early volumes of verse, which contained a fair number of pæans to young men, had all appeared in privately printed editions. Sydney Oswald, cherished in Uranian circles for his translation of the twelfth book of *The Greek Anthology*, privately printed in 1914 and replete with pederastic verse, appeared in one of the earliest anthologies of war verse, *Soldier Poets: Songs of the Fighting Men*, published in 1916. His poem 'The dead soldier', which utilizes conventional romantic terms with no sense of irony or concession to the changed sex of the subject, clearly would not have been acceptable to the general public under any other circumstances. These poets were not only shielded by the patriotic necessity of celebrating 'fallen heroes', but also by a tradition of memorial poetry stretching back in English literature to Milton's 'Lycidas', Shelley's 'Adonaïs' and Tennyson's 'In Memoriam'. The poems in the section THE DEAD are intended to display how the tradition of memorial verse was infused by the spirit of the First World War, which enabled poets like Sassoon, Oswald and Geoffrey Faber to feed poems on male love to an unsuspecting public. Faber, however, was careful not to overstep the bounds of acceptable taste. He retained his most overt poems, including the sonnet sequence 'Specimen of agony' which charts a wartime love affair, for the collected edition of 1941, appropriately entitled *The Buried Stream*.

The most influential of the great memorial poems was, of course, Tennyson's 'In memoriam', and its fiercely elegiac tone was echoed by many First World War poets. Most notably by Wilfred Owen in

'Futility', which echoes its famous despairing section LVI beginning 'So careful of the type? but no'; and most obviously by Maurice Baring, whose poem to Auberon Herbert, Captain Lord Lucas was appropriately entitled 'In memoriam A.H.' The beginning of Baring's poem:

> The wind had blown away the rain
> That all day long had soaked the level plain.
> Against the horizon's fiery wrack,
> The sheds loomed black.[57]

clearly reflects the predominant 'ghastly thro' the drizzling rain . . . breaks the blank day' mood of Tennyson's poem. Published in 1850, 'In memoriam' was received initially with caution, especially by the critic of *The Times* who pointed out that the undertones of the poem were rather unconventional. It was, however, given the royal seal of approval by Queen Victoria, who presumably skated over the depths and applied the general drift to her own situation as a widow. Much of the poem's imagery is that of conventional love, with Tennyson describing himself in terms of a widower, but this is undercut by a less conventional emotional tone indicated by the phrase 'loved deeplier, darklier understood' and the incantatory refrain 'mine, mine forever, ever mine'. Brian Reade has remarked that 'the fact that Tennyson evolved an emphatically heterosexual image later in life does nothing to disqualify him as homosexual when he wrote 'In memoriam', or in that part of his temperament he kept sensitive to the memory of Hallam.'[58] This could be equally be said of many of the First World War poets, who retained an intense affection for an 'Arthur Hallam' many years after the war had ended. Eric Hiscock wrote of his friend Brook: 'Ours was a pure love, where neither refused the other anything if it was wanted. Selfless, flame-like, it burned in me long after that day I heard he was dead, and even now I can conjure up his face, serene, beautiful, pure.'[59]

Whether the expression of love in these poems was intended to be platonic or sexual, it was all, nevertheless, the expression of some kind of love; and the intensities of emotion involved render them suitable for inclusion under the banner of homo-eroticism. The emotional pull of poetry expressing the camaraderie of the trenches was such that those not directly involved in the conflict – civilian poets like Thomas Hardy and non-combatant soldier poets like Wilfred Gibson – were drawn to the idea. Even some women poets like Eva Mudocci, masquerading for verisimilitude under the name of Harry Brander, felt impelled to contribute to the tradition. Neither should we forget that one of the impulses behind '*The Waste Land*' was the death by drowning at Gallipoli of T. S. Eliot's close friend, the French poet Jean Verdenal, commemorated in the section 'Death by Water':

> O you who turn the wheel and look to windward,
> Consider Phlebas, who was once as handsome and tall as you.[60]

War poetry cannot really be said to have existed before the First World War, largely because for the first time the emerging voices were actually serving soldiers. *Drummer Hodge: Poetry of the Boer War* by Malvern van Wyck Smith reveals that although a great deal of poetry was written about the Boer War, both from a patriotic and a pacifist angle, little of the combatant verse is memorable. Hardy's 'Drummer Hodge', perhaps the finest poem to emerge from the Boer War, is a tender and moving elegy to a representative soldier, but it lacks the intensity of Owen's 'Futility', because Hardy lacked both Owen's temperament and experience. Of particular interest to the theme of this anthology are two poems quoted by van Wyck Smith, written by Austin Ferrand for his fellow Oxford undergraduate, the Decadent poet Lionel Johnson:

> I feel the battery of rushing blood
> Drown us again in the resistless flood
> Of overpowering passion, undenied
> And unregretted. You are by my side,
> Laid on my heart, through the surging night,
> Till with dawn you fade from touch and sight.[61]

Ferrand's poems were published in the periodical *Outlook* after his death in South Africa in September 1900. Van Wyck Smith remarks that 'the two poems addressed to Johnson represent a powerful voice which was either unique among campaign poets or, for obvious reasons, suppressed in all other cases.'[62] What was a rarity in the Boer War became a commonplace in the First World War, and although there are many poems from the Boer War on the theme of comradeship, they have none of the power of the poems from the later conflict.

There appears to have been a general reluctance in Victorian England to face the full realities of war, although there was an abundance of verse celebrating the deeds of heroism, past and present, a tradition that continued into the First World War with poets like Alfred Austin, Henry Newbolt and Laurence Binyon. The most notable exceptions to this tradition were Thomas Hardy, Rudyard Kipling and A. E. Housman. Although the irony of *The Dynasts* and *Satires of Circumstances* came to influence poets like Sassoon later in the war, the primary and most pervasive influences on the poets of the First World War were undoubtedly Kipling and Housman, two late-Victorian writers who chose as their predominant subjects, although with strikingly different approaches, war and the military. Indeed, their most famous works, respectively *Barrack-Room Ballads* (1892) and *A Shropshire Lad* (1896), could almost be said to have anticipated the First World War, in that their principal themes of the camaraderie and the mortality of soldiers were to become the notes most frequently struck by later poets.

Correlli Barnett has written that during the eighteenth century 'soldiering reached the low place in British society it was to occupy until the Great War in 1914, an occupation despised by the middle and working classes as a disgrace hardly less than prison.'[63] But as the growth of the Empire became a major item of national policy, the status of the soldier as crusader for the Imperial Mission improved. By the time of the Boer War the soldier had become something of a national hero; with the First World War he became a saint. Kipling, more than anyone, enhanced the standing of the soldier, largely by shaming the Victorian public with the revelation of their hypocrisy:

> For it's Tommy this, an' Tommy that, an'
> 'Chuck him out, the brute!'
> But it's 'Saviour of 'is country' when the
> guns begin to shoot.[64]

Kipling's experiences in the Indian Civil Service gave him an unprecedented insight both into the workings of the British Army and into the life of that previously unsung hero 'Tommy Atkins'. Using the idiom of the music hall, street ballad and barrack-room, he provided a common vocabulary by which an honest view of soldiering could be communicated. Although this became something of a cliché when treated by later and lesser hands, he presented through his novels and poetry an unprecedented image of a profane and rough, but courageous and honest soldier, which forced the public into an appreciation of those who had formerly been considered the dregs of society:

> We aren't no thin red 'eroes, nor we aren't no blackguards too,
> But single men in barracks, most remarkable like you;
> An' if sometimes our conduck isn't all your fancy paints:
> Why, single men in barracks don't grow into plaster saints.[65]

Kipling's accounts of male courage and devotion to duty in a world without women were enormously successful, and were part of a popular culture that included writers like G. A. Henty and Rider Haggard. The cult of self-sufficient masculinity propagated by these writers constitutes a school of male romance, where women are redundant and camaraderie is the essential value. Henty was the most popular boy's writer of his day, producing eighty-two titles between 1871 and 1906. His stories range from pre-Christian times to the Boer War, but they are all essentially the same story. Regardless of period or place, his characters are instantly recognizable as late-Victorian public-school boys, upright and honest, not to say priggish, and ready to fight for the Cause, which invariably sounds like the British Empire. The hero usually has a companion, sometimes a brother or friend but more often a social or racial 'inferior', a relationship that reflects the recognition of class and race on which the Empire was based. Unsurprisingly, his heroes show little interest in girls, who are usually relegated to the end of the story as the heroes' reward, the real value of which resides in their property rather than their sex.

Henty's popularity and influence were equally considerable. He boasted that 'many boys have joined the cadets and afterwards gone into the army through reading my stories'.[66] Generations of schoolboys were raised on Henty, and came to believe that the 'civilizing' effect of the British Empire was reason enough for its expansion and ample justification for its interference into the affairs of other nations. As one critic complained: 'After fourteen or fifteen years' perusal of "piffle" written apparently for his edification, the young Englishman leaves home and country with the very firm idea that, he, personally, is equal to two or more Frenchmen, about four Germans, an indefinite number of Russians, and any quantity you care to mention of the remaining scum of the earth.'[67]

Those who read Henty as schoolboys would have graduated to Haggard as adults. *King Solomon's Mines* and *She*, published in 1886 and 1887 respectively, stimulated an adult taste for exotic adventure stories, and the male romance became one of the dominant forms of the late-Victorian period. The same ingredients are in Haggard as in Henty, although Haggard is more consistently contemporary, and his stories are consequently more obviously imperial allegories. Their principal difference, unsurprisingly, is on the subject of women. In Henty females are largely innocuous (and pre-pubertal); but in Haggard they can be positively dangerous, and worse, a threat to the central male relationship. The heroines of *She*, *Nada the Lily* and *Cleopatra* are all powerful foreign women (English women present no such problem) whose sexual identities are not only a threat to male supremacy but also to the conveniently associated values of Western civilization. Interestingly, another such heroine, Marqueda in *Queen Sheba's Ring*, is tamed by the effortless superiority of the English hero, for whom she abandons her kingdom. The romances of Henty and Haggard were an influential part of the education and leisure of many future soldiers, and the comradeships at the heart of these fantasies of Africa, India and the ancient world were to become a terrible reality on the Western Front, where the justness of the Cause no longer seemed enough to guarantee victory, and where there could be no dependence on an eventual happy ending.

Kipling was never as fantastic as his contemporaries, as well as being rather more democratic. In works like *Soldiers Three* and *The Man Who Would be King* he demonstrated that romantic friendships were not the preserve of officers and could be found among the other ranks. This effectively enlarged the emotional capacity, and consequently the dignity, of working-class literary figures to an unprecedented degree. The language and locations of Kipling's novels, dramatic lyrics and monologues have a cogency that those of his contemporaries lack, and as Charles Carrington has observed: 'Search English literature and you will find no treatment of the English soldier on an adequate scale between Shakespeare and Kipling.'[68] He was also responsible for establishing the tone and character of a new kind of poetry, thus setting a valuable precedent for the poets of First World War. His influence is most apparent in poems like Gilbert Frankau's 'How Rifleman Brown came to Valhalla' and G. A. Studdert Kennedy's 'His mate' in particular, and the poems in the section MATES in general.

By the outbreak of the First World War Kipling's verse had deteriorated from the markedly anti-imperialistic poems of *Barrack-Room Ballads* and *Departmental Ditties*, concerned with people rather than ideas, to the admonitory declarations of *The Seven Seas* and *The Five Nations*, dealing in political abstractions and moral imperatives. His most successful First World War poem is 'My boy Jack', which laments the death of his son who went missing in action in 1916. The emotional power of this poem is remarkable for a poet whose principal failing lies in his characters' inability to express intense emotions such as love or grief, which render them tongue-tied or maudlin, except in those cases where approaching death loosens the bonds of class and rank. As Kipling was to discover, in the First World War such cases were to become the rule rather than the exception:

> 'Have you heard of My boy Jack?'
>   Not this tide.
> 'When d'you think he'll come back?'
>   Not with this wind and this tide.[69]

The want of emotion in Kipling is supplied in abundance by Housman. *A Shropshire Lad* provided the poets of the First World War with a complete register of emotions about young soldiers, their friendships, their injuries, their bravery, and their deaths:

On yonder island, not to rise,
  Never to stir forth free.
Far from his folk a dead lad lies
  That once was friends with me.

Lie you easy, dream you light,
  And sleep you fast for aye;
And luckier may you find the night
  Than ever you found the day.[70]

Above all else is Housman's gift of the word 'lad', which his poems qualify as 'the handsome of face and the handsome of heart . . . that will die in their glory and never be old'.[71] A more accurate First World War term would probably be 'batty', which David Jones defines as 'a most intimate companion. Jonathan was certainly David's "batty".'[72] But the term 'lad' was more evocative, as Paul Fussell has observed: 'In Great War diction there are three degrees of erotic heat attaching to three words: "men" is largely neutral; "boys" is a little warmer; "lads" is very warm . . . As "men" grow more attractive, they are seen as "boys", until finally, when conceived as potential lovers, they turn into "lads".'[73]

Robert Graves realized that 'poor Housman had a passion for soldiers', but nonetheless thought that there was no 'vain posturing in Housman; the verse is almost painfully clean and in perfect good faith'.[74] Although Housman did not have Kipling's authority of experience, it was with the war that *A Shropshire Lad* became really popular, and the seductive fatalism of the image of the soldier as victim of an inevitably tragic confrontation between man and circumstance had never before seemed so apposite. According to Robert Nichols *A Shropshire Lad* was 'in every pocket' just before the war, and became accessible to all when some of the poems were printed as a broadsheet for the troops by *The Times*.[75] It was also one of the books Sassoon took overseas with him. Few First World War poets were immune to Housman's influence, and many poems, particularly those of Richard Dennys, J. D. Greenway and others in the YOUTH IN ARMS section read like rogue pieces from *A Shropshire Lad*. This is a remarkable feat for a work that, in Brian Reade's words, 'is like a beautiful ruin built over an invisible framework, and Housman obscured the framework so well that until relatively recently not many readers of the poems seemed to guess that it was "*l'amour de l'impossible*" which haunted many of them.'[76] This could almost as aptly be said for the poetry of the First World War, although we may wish to replace '*l'amour de l'impossible*' with '*l'amour de l'incroyable*'.

Paul Fussell suggests that First World War poetry falls into a tradition of homo-erotic verse, rising from the Aesthetic movement and passing through the Uranian poets (who celebrated pederasty) to the war poets. He qualifies his thesis with the admission that, 'It is impossible to say how widely known the work of the Uranians was. Although some of it was circulated "privately", most was quite public. If it could not be said that their performances created an atmosphere favourable to a wider homo-erotic concept of soldiering, they are at least an indication of what was in the air.'[77] Sassoon and Owen knew C. K. Scott Moncrieff and Philip Bainbrigge, authors of Uranian material, and Sassoon had corresponded with the most popular Uranian poet John Gambril Nicholson, author of *Love in Earnest*, but there is little evidence that they were influenced by the Uranian tradition, which in any case celebrated boys rather than lads. Owen's relationship with the schoolboy Vivian Rampton while a lay assistant at Dunsden Vicarage in 1912, however, had distinct Uranian overtones, although he could not at that date have been aware of any supportive literary tradition. Geoffrey Faber, at least, appears to have been acquainted with the poetry of Lord Alfred Douglas. The fifth sonnet in the 'Specimen of agony' sequence refers to 'the grief that has no name', a clear echo of 'the love that dare not speak its name' from 'The two loves'. Another Douglas poem, 'Rejected', and 'The two loves' are also echoed in 'Love and Fate', written in 1920, where 'Fate' forbids 'Love' entry into the garden, just as 'True Love' challenged 'Shame' in Douglas' poem:

I saw love lying by the gate,
   The cruel shackles fast on every limb.
And all his look was fastened upon fate,
   But fate said nothing to him.[78]

At least the First World War, which had seen 'the love that dare not speak its name' achieve an unprecedented volubility, ensured the passage of 'Shame' to 'Love', and 'True Love' to 'Fate'.

Fussell further insists that 'long before the war the Uranians were producing poems that were at first glance indistinguishable from poems of the Great War. This they did by placing before themselves and their readers the most moving image they could think of – the sudden death of boys.'[79] Although something of this emerges in Ackerley's admission that 'Many a handsome farm- or tradesboy was to be found in the ranks of one's command, and to a number of beautiful but untouchable NCOs and privates did I allot an early sentimental or heroic death in my nauseous verse',[80] the poets of the First World War had no real need of such ruses, nor for any of the Uranian ways of evasion, such as classical fancy dress, by which unpalatable themes could be presented to the public. The war had legitimized the celebration of male youth and beauty.

Few of the noted Uranian poets writing during the First World War seem to have taken advantage of an audience sympathetic to images of war featuring beautiful but doomed young men. Edmund John, the author of *A Flute of Sardonyx*, in his wartime publication *The Wind in the Temple* includes only three war poems: 'In memoriam' to the memory of Lord Roberts, 'Ave Indi' on the Indian contribution to the war effort, and 'The Huns 1914', a rhymed version of the Bryce Report. The lack of Uranian interest in the erotic possibilities of war becomes clear in F. S. Woodley's *A Crown of Friendship* which contains both Uranian and war poems, celebrating respectively the themes of pederasty and comradeship. The shift in emphasis and the dimunition in erotic heat between the two themes suggest that for poets like Woodley soldiers were not boys, and therefore the focus of sexual interest, but men, and rather the object of sympathetic identification. The same distinction can be found in the work of a poet mentioned by Eric Hiscock in *The Bells of Hell go Ting-a-ling-a-ling*. As a boy in Oxford, Hiscock was friends with an undergraduate pseudonymously called Oldham. At their last meeting before Oldham went to France, Hiscock remembers:

> Oldham, alas, was full of love. It was a love that found no reciprocation from the rather callous schoolboy whose thoughts had already turned to long-legged, pig-tailed flappers in short skirts . . . He pleaded with his passenger in the smoothly flowing punt to be allowed a fugitive male kiss before the war took him away from any hope of such delights, and he was resolutely repulsed.[81]

From the poems quoted by Hiscock, it emerges that Oldham was, in fact, 'Rex' Freston, author of the poems 'To A.M.' and 'The mess table'. Hiscock's inside information shades to a rather darker complexion the undedicated love poems in *The Quest of Truth*:

> So did I love your soul: but after years
> Of loving that strange sweetness, that I knew
> Was your true self, I longed to kiss your lips,
> Your hands, your hair: I loved your body too.[82]

Hiscock also remembers overhearing Oldham tell his parents, 'I want to love your son honourably and well.'[83] The poems, however, suggest a more ambiguous motive. 'Despair (To—)', quoted above, reveals that such high-mindedness was impossible to sustain, and although appreciation of the 'soul' was the avowed, and probably sincere, intention, it inevitably led to a desire of the 'body'. The anonymously dedicated sequence of poems 'To—' in Freston's pre-service volume of poetry *The Quest of Beauty*, reveals the unhappiness of one who bears a love unacceptable to himself and to society, from which the only refuge is death. The last poem in the sequence, 'When the dust and toil is over', anticipates Freston's subsequent death and burial in France.

Freston's Uranian poems are full of coded terms like 'strange', 'sweetness', 'shame', 'sorrow' and 'curious tenderness' which firmly locate them in the tradition of homo-erotic verse. But in Freston's hands, as in those of Woodley, the tradition does not inform upon the poems of war, and it took greater poets, like Owen and Sassoon, to write war poetry through the combined forces of a literary tradition and a sexual persuasion.

Peter Parker in *The Old Lie* convincingly suggests that the work of the Uranians was less influential than the widely read popular school stories that celebrated romantic friendships:

> Part of the reason that school stories seem a more likely influence upon poetry of the Great War than Uranian verse is the question of tone. There is something at once arch and furtive about Uranian poetry which is not noticeable in school novels and is entirely absent in the frank, open poetry of the war.[84]

Although the novels of Haggard and Henty are likely to have reached an even wider audience than those of the public-school stories, certainly the emotional tone of First World War poetry, largely written by public-school officers, owes much to novels like *Tim* (1891), *The Hill* (1905) and *David Blaize* (1916). A letter to E. F. Benson from a major in the army testifies to the influence of novels like *David Blaize*:

> I have just been reading *David Blaize* and think it lovely – the best school story yet written bar none. Here we have a continual stream of young officers to train as scouts and snipers and there has been a great run on David, as many as three copies of him on one course. Many of the lads that come have few if any memories of anything but home and school as this is a young man's job. I think you would perhaps like to know the pleasure your book has given to these very fine and gallant lads who come first to army training school from the trenches.[85]

Of the famous public-school stories, *The Hill* is the most passionate, probably because the author Horace Annesley Vachell had more reason to write unselfconsciously than either Howard Sturgis or E. F. Benson. It is also the most prescient, for at the end of novel the hero leaves school to take part in the Boer War, where he meets a hero's death. Vachell had succeeded in not only anticipating, but perhaps also precipitating, the careers of many First World War officers.

The effect of writers like Haggard and Henty, and Vachell and Erskine Childers (whose novel *The Riddle of the Sands*, published in 1903, features a pair of Oxford graduates successfully defending Britain against an imminent German invasion) was to encourage a frame of mind receptive to the idea of war and to the attendant qualities of comradeship, heroism and patriotism. A less pervasive, but perhaps more incisive, influence on the poets of the period was Edward Carpenter. Sassoon visited Carpenter in 1911, admitting that *The Intermediate Sex* had opened up a new life for him; and Graves wrote to him from Charterhouse in 1914, confessing that *Iolaus* and *The Intermediate Sex* had taken the scales from his eyes and crystallized his vague feelings. Many others would have been acquainted with his gospel of 'the soul of comradeship' through his most famous work,

Towards Democracy. Published in four parts from 1883–1905, the poem is a celebration of comradeship between rustic youths uncorrupted by civilization; and his image of the ideal comrade, 'the thick-thighed hot coarse-fleshed young bricklayer with a strap around his waist', was the prototype of many First World War characters, including Sassoon's Jim Linthwaite.[86] With *Towards Democracy* Carpenter helped to evolve a language of male love that although discreet, distinguished it from the conventions of heterosexual love, and his poetic influence can be observed in Harold Monro's volumes, *Before Dawn* (1911), *Children of Love* (1914) and *Strange Meetings* (1917), which in turn influenced Wilfred Owen in such poems as 'The time was aeon' and 'Strange meeting'. More direct in their message than *Towards Democracy* were *Homogenic Love* and *The Intermediate Sex*, published in 1895 and 1908, two of the first English publications to advocate the recognition and acceptance of homosexual men and women.

The effect of Carpenter's work on the minds of many confused individuals is incalculable, but it must have been at least comparable to the effect of the work of Walt Whitman on Carpenter. Whitman's philosophy of 'the institution of the dear love of comrades' first emerged with the initial publication of *Leaves of Grass* in 1855.[87] His commitment to his beliefs led to his work among the wounded in the American Civil War, and his experiences gave rise to a second volume of verse, *Drum Taps*, published in 1863. Significantly, *Drum Taps* was republished in Britain in 1915, with an introduction reprinted from *The Times Literary Supplement* which stressed the relevance of the poems to the present conflict. Carpenter saw in Whitman's belief in 'adhesiveness' a means of spiritualizing a materialist society and of bringing the classes together, a message he propagated in *Towards Democracy* which was begun after visiting Whitman in 1877. The concept of 'adhesiveness' as a binding agent of society had obvious validity in the circumstances of war, where comradeship was a necessity for survival. Ernest Rhys found that whenever he tried to express his feelings about the war he was drawn inevitably to Whitman, and Whitman's work was also admired by such soldier-poets as Siegfried Sassoon, Ivor Gurney, Harold Monro, Edward Thomas and Isaac Rosenberg.

The most obvious omission from this anthology is, of course, Isaac

Rosenberg. As a working-class Jew he was immune to the social and literary traditions that influenced most of the poets of the First World War, and as a soldier he seems to have found more comfort in his poetry than in his comrades. Rosenberg's remark, 'I am determined that this war, with all its powers for devastation, shall not master my poeting,' suggests a dedication to his craft that reached beyond the pressure of his circumstances, and unlike most of the poets under discussion he achieves his effects through a compassionate detachment from, rather than a compassionate identification with, his subject.[88] A close examination of the final image from 'Dead man's dump' reveals how Rosenberg moves away from a particular to a universal response to the death of a fellow soldier, which diffuses the sensuousness of the situation, but without diminishing any of the power:

So we crashed round the bend,
We heard his weak scream,
We heard his very last sound,
As our wheels grazed his dead face.[89]

Owen and Sassoon best exemplify the attitude of compassionate identification, and their achievement is a testimony to the effectiveness of their literary and social heritage. For not only were Owen and Sassoon by nature of their poetic gifts at the centre of the homo-erotic poetic tradition, they were also acquainted with the remnants of Wilde's circle – Robbie Ross, More Adey, and Robert Sherard – as well as with other sympathetic figures like Harold Monro and Osbert Sitwell. Before the war Sassoon had published several volumes of verse closely modelled on Swinburne, and like Owen he was at heart a late Romantic with a taste for melancholy lyricism:

I listen for him through the rain,
And on the dusk of starless hours,
I know that he will return again;
Loth he was to forsake me.
He comes with glimmering of flowers
And stir of music to awake me.[90]

Although the theme of Sassoon's poetry did not change with the coming of war, the context did, and Sassoon found it necessary to abandon his Decadent posturing for a more direct form of expression. His poem 'Conscripts' is both a valediction to the *Songs* of the past and a recognition of the virtues of the present, as well as charting the development in his affections from gilded youth to common soldier:

Their training done, I shipped them all to France,
Where most of them I'd loved too long got killed.
Rapture and pale Enchantment and Romance,
And many a sickly, slender lord who'd filled
My soul long since with lutanies of sin,
Went home, because they couldn't stand the din.

But the kind, common ones that I despised
(Hardly a man of them I'd count as friend),
What stubborn-hearted virtues they disguised!
They stood and played the hero to the end,
Won gold and silver medals bright with bars,
And marched resplendent home with crowns and stars.[91]

Among the books Sassoon took to Egypt in February 1918 was Walter Pater's *Studies in the History of the Renaissance*. Pater, who provided the Decadent handbook with *Marius the Epicurean* in 1885, had written in *Studies* . . . in 1873: 'While all melts under our feet, we may well catch at any exquisite passion, or any contribution to knowledge that seems, by a lifted horizon, to set the spirit free for a moment, or any stirring of the senses, strange dyes, strange flowers, and curious odours, or work of the artist's hands, or the face of one's friend.'[92] In a few succinct words Pater anticipated not only the development in literature from Aestheticism to Decadence, but also the circumstances under which friendships were made in the trenches of the First World War.

The principal impulse behind the Decadent movement was the pursuit of sensation. In a world grown increasingly materialist and conventional, only through sensation could beauty, the goal of art, be found unsullied. It was therefore necessary that the artist, the mediator of beauty, should have exquisitely tuned nerves, capable of registering with intensity and accuracy all sensations, painful or pleasurable. In the pursuit of sensation there developed, unsurprisingly, an attraction to all forms of 'deviant' behaviour. In life this meant Swinburne and *le vice anglais*, and Wilde and his 'feasting with panthers', and in literature, the proliferation of images of death, madness, suffering, martyrdom, murder, blood, terror and illicit sexuality. For both Sassoon and Owen, before they began to move in circles where the subject was openly discussed, the only intellectual acknowledgement of homosexuality they would have encountered would have been as one of the 'strange sins' of the Decadence. Their late-Romantic heritage would have seemed even more relevant when they arrived at the front, for they would have found in the circumstances of modern warfare a tangible realization of the nightmares of Decadent literature. Both these influences are focused in the image of St Sebastian, a particular favourite of Decadent writers and painters, and characterized by Wilde as possessing 'all the pathetic uselessness of martyrdom, all its wasted beauty', a sentiment especially appropriate to the circumstances of death in the trenches.[93] A safer symbol of homo-erotic contemplation than Christ, St Sebastian was to be found transposed to the trenches and dressed in khaki in such poems as Owen's 'Asleep' and Sassoon's 'The dug-out'.

But the pursuit of sensation was a dangerous game, and fear of retribution of the kind subsequently meted out to Wilde led many Decadent writers towards discretion rather than exposition. There developed as a result, as we have seen with the soldier-poet 'Rex' Freston, the use of a special vocabulary of words like 'exquisite', 'secret', 'strange', 'sin', 'smile' and 'mystery', which helped to produce an aura of exclusivity and the concept of a secret knowledge only to be understood by the initiated. This concept was to find a parallel in the feelings of men who had fought at the front. Charles Carrington wrote: 'We are still an initiate generation, possessing a secret that can never be communicated . . . Twenty million of us . . . shared the experience with one another but with no one else, and are what we are because, in that war, we were soldiers.'[94] Sassoon reiterated Carrington's remark with the comment that those who had fought were 'carrying something in our heads that belongs to us alone, and to those we left behind in battle'.[95] This exclusive and incommunicable secret is 'the truth untold' in Owen's 'Strange Meeting' and the 'proud-surging melodies of joy' in Sassoon's 'Secret Music'. Thus, the roots of the belief that all who served in the war carried with pride an indelible mark discernible only by those that had shared the experience can, particularly in the work of Owen and Sassoon, be traced to the attempts by Decadent writers to cloak their homosexuality.

For many artists steeped in Decadent conventions, the search for exquisite sensations and the rejection of orthodox moral constraints led to a spiritual ennui and a disgust at contemporary society, and poets like Rupert Brooke and Robert Nichols welcomed the outbreak of war in 1914 as a chance for regeneration. In 'Peace' Brooke wrote of war as a refuge for those 'who have known shame' and that the participants in the coming struggle were 'swimmers into cleanness leaping'. But Brooke's public appeal had a private resonance, and as Paul Delaney observes: 'The war let [Brooke] feel that the whole nation had joined him in spurning homosexual and pacifist Bloomsbury. What the common reader could not know, however, was that Rupert hated Bloomsbury for its complicity with his own sexual guilt, and that this was what it would take a war to wash off.'[96] For Nichols too, the war appears to have been a public resolution to a private situation, and the answer to his prayer for a 'power to quick with life the smouldered wick again'.[97] The poems in *Ardours and Endurances*, read in sequence, form a narrative in which the poet, tired and shamed by an excess of 'passion', escapes from the cloying attractions of women to the intensity of male relationships at the front.

Owen, who had had a more thoroughgoing grounding in Decadent literature than any of his contemporaries, having studied the originals while working in France rather than depending on English pasticheurs like Swinburne, never abandoned his late-Romantic heritage, and produced recognizably Decadent poems throughout the war. 'Has your soul sipped' is of the tradition, and it develops a sequence of lush comparisons of 'sweetness' culminating in the 'sweetest' of all images:

> that smile
> Faint as a wan, worn myth,
> Faint and exceeding small
> On a boy's murdered mouth.[98]

This poem was written at Craiglockhart in July 1917, when Owen was also making his first forays into poetic realism under the influence of Sassoon. Having served at the front, Owen, by this stage, was only too aware of the realities of pain and death, and the poem 'I saw his round mouth's crimson as it fell' is a conscious attempt to shape his literary tastes to accommodate his new experiences. Dominic Hibberd observes: 'Most of Owen's mature poems have their origins in his earlier verse because the development from love poetry to war poetry was an expression of his whole self, including his knowledge of literature. He took the twilight of the Decadence out of dream and fantasy and related it to history.'[99] In Owen's hands the Decadent clichés take on a new and truly terrible life. The sentimental fantasy of Wilde's 'Wasted days':

> A fair slim boy not made for this world's pain,
> With hair of gold thick clustering round his ears.[100]

is revised by Owen in 'Arms and the Boy' as;

> And God will grow no talons at his heels,
> Nor antlers through the thickness of his curls.

One of Owen's last poems, 'The kind ghosts', features an archetypal *femme fatale* who is unaware of the pain and death she brings her lovers. But the sleeping figure is also Britannia, whose security depends upon the unseen sacrifice of her young men. In such poems Owen achieves a successful fusion of an established literary form with a wholly contemporary significance.

At a less profound level than with Owen, Decadent literature for many was represented by poems about beautiful youths and unspecified, but fairly obvious, sins. Owen was certainly adept in this vein, as his poem 'I am the ghost of Shadwell Stairs' reveals. This poem has usually been interpreted as an impressionistic piece about a prostitute, along the lines of Wilde's 'Impression du Matin'. C. K. Scott Moncrieff, however, recalled turning the poem into rhymed French prose, resulting in a rather different interpretation: 'I give the first verse, on account of the last word, which Owen welcomed as tho' it put the key to the whole ... "*Je suis le petit revenant du Bassin; le long de quai, par l'abreuvoir, et dans l'immode abbatoir j'y pietine, ombre fantassin.*"'[101] Owen has gone beyond the Decadent use of the prostitute as a symbol of homosexuality, and has instead cast himself, a *fantassin* or infantryman, in the central role. The basis of this poem was probably a return visit by Owen to the East End of London where he had seen, before his enlistment in 1915, a boy of surpassing beauty, the subject of 'Lines to a beauty seen in Limehouse'.

Owen was not only influenced by the late Romantics, but also by early Romantics like Wordsworth, Keats and, in particular, Shelley, 'the greatest genius of our time', whose political idealism, social conscience, religious atheism and anti-militarism were a sound education for a future war poet.[102] The humanitarian values of the early Romantics enabled Owen to judge war as a wholly destructive phenomenon, while the late-Romantic obsessions with martyrdom and homosexuality made it a profoundly moving experience.

Owen's real gift was to forge from his own literary and personal interests an approach to the war that was both universal and intimate, and one fully adequate to the demands of his subject. His approach was also unique in that, as Bernard Bergonzi observes, unlike Sassoon, Blunden and Graves, Owen 'rarely attempts a contrast, nostalgic or ironic, between the trenches and remembered English scenes'.[103] Instead, he concentrates on the physiques and feelings of the soldiers around him until he achieves an almost sensual identification with them, the lesson of negative capability learned well from his idol Keats. In poems like 'Disabled' he achieves an immediacy that almost amounts to possession, and which reveals an absolute commitment to his subject. Owen's devotion to his men was not only a literary one, and his conception of his role as a poet and as a soldier was identical. He wrote to his mother after he had returned to the front in the autumn of 1918: 'I came out in order to help these boys – directly by leading them as well as an officer can; indirectly, by watching their suffering that I may speak of them as a pleader can. I have done the first.'[104] His poems are a testament as to how well he succeeded with the second.

Owen's poems emphasize the completeness and the exclusivity of the relationships made in the trenches, which he raises to such a pitch of intensity that they both disqualify and transcend romantic love.

Having used the poetry of romantic love as a model, it was inevitable that it should come to be seen by the soldier-poets as an inadequate vehicle for the expression of the new love between comrades; and women, the subject of traditional romantic poetry, became as obsolete as the form itself. As Conrad, Ackerley's hero in *The Prisoners of War*, remarks when questioned by Madame Louis, 'I have heard you do not like much the fair sex,' – 'The fair sex? Which sex is that?'[105]

The poems in the section THE GREATER LOVE show how the relationships forged in the trenches came, implicitly or directly, to challenge the primacy of heterosexual love. For with the overwhelming need for soldiers to focus all their emotions on their comrades, heterosexual love lost its sway, and although many of the poems are not homosexual in a sexual sense, they are, nevertheless, the products of imaginations for whom, at least at that time, the female image had no potency. Nichols essays a straightforward contrast between conventional romance and the love of comrades in 'Fulfilment', while in 'Greater love' Owen mounts a thorough demolition of heterosexual emotion. Some poets went beyond the simple comparisons of Nichols and others, and struggled to redefine and relocate traditional love-lyrics in the new circumstances of war. In Robert Graves's 'Two Fusiliers', the imagery, as in the poetry of romantic love, is drawn from the minutiae of the shared life of the 'lovers', namely the trenches, the mud and the blood of the Western Front. Owen further develops this redefinition of love in terms of the trench experience, to a relocation of love. In 'Apologia pro poemate meo', he denies that love and beauty are as 'old song' have described them, and affirms they are now only to be found with the soldiers at the front.

Although many women served with distinction at the front as well at home, they were too closely identified with the civilian ethos that promoted the war to receive any sympathy from the war poets. As Cecil Day-Lewis remarked apropos Owen: '[He] had no pity to spare for the suffering of bereaved women,'; and in Ford Madox Ford's *Parade's End* (1924–28) and Richard Aldington's *Death of a Hero* (1929) the sexual lies of wives were seen as a complement to the public lies of the establishment.[106] To the men at the front, the most apparent images of women were the recruiting chorines, the ladies handing out white feathers to men not in uniform, who were often men on leave or invalided out of the forces, and the 'Little Mother' whose letter to the *Morning Post* is quoted by Graves in *Goodbye to All That*:

> Our ears are not deaf to the cry that is ever ascending from the battlefield from our men of flesh and blood whose indomitable courage is borne to us, so to speak, on every blast of the wind. We women pass on the human ammunition of 'only sons' to fill up the gaps, so that when the 'common soldier' looks back before 'going over the top' he may see the women of the British race at his heels, reliable, dependent, uncomplaining.[107]

These images of blind patriotism were strenuously promoted by the propagandists (usually male), who were responsible for, amongst other things, such songs (invariably sung by women) as 'We don't want to lose you but we think you ought to go', 'Be a soldier be a man', 'I'm glad my son grew up to be a soldier' and most notoriously 'I'll make a man of you'. Other songs, like 'Take me back to dear old Blighty' and 'It's a long long trail', did express the very real longing for peace shared by all soldiers, but they were hopelessly out of touch with the realities of life at the front. It should be remembered, however, that the composer of the most popular of First World War songs, at the front as well as at home, was none other than Ivor Novello:

> Keep the home fires burning,
> Though your hearts are yearning,
> Though your lads are far away
> They dream of home.[108]

But the soldiers' much-cherished dreams of home were often soured when men on leave found an England ignorant of the conditions in France and oblivious of their true feelings. Robert Graves thought that 'England looked strange to us returned soldiers. We could not understand the war-madness that ran wild everywhere, looking for a pseudo-military outlet. The civilians talked a foreign language; and it was a newspaper language.'[109] Many soldiers felt guilty at leaving their comrades behind and could not wait to return to the trenches. Sassoon wrote: 'And still the memory of the Company haunts me and wrings my heart and I hear them saying, "When's the Captain coming back?" It seems as if there's nothing to go back to in England as long as the War goes on.'[110] These feelings of guilt and alienation are expressed by the poems in the BACK HOME section.

The power of identification between soldiers was such that as feelings of alienation from England increased, so a sympathy with enemy soldiers developed, as the poems in the section THE ENEMY reveal. All soldiers, whatever their nationality, were seen as victims of the war, the politicians at home and the unthinking civilian ethos. The intensity of Henry Williamson's sympathy with the individual German soldier in the First World War, whose cries of '*Mutter, Mutter*' could be heard coming from the enemy trenches, led him to embrace Fascism in the post-war years and to deify Hitler as 'the great man across the Rhine'. When on sick-leave in England, Sassoon developed a 'Secret antagonism to all uncomplimentary references to the German Army', and he decided on his return to France in May 1918 that his purpose was no longer to kill Germans but only to look after his men.[111] The change in Sassoon's feelings had begun with the sight of a dead German soldier:

> As I stepped over one of the Germans an impulse made me lift him up from the miserable ditch. Propped against the bank, his blond face was undisfigured, except by mud which I wiped from his eyes and mouth with my coat sleeve. He'd evidently been killed while digging, for his tunic was loosely knotted about his shoulders. He didn't look to be more than eighteen. Hoisting him a little higher, I thought what a gentle face he had, and I remembered that this was the first time I had touched one of our enemies with my hands. Perhaps I had some dim sense of the futility which had put an end to this good-looking youth.[112]

The pervasiveness of the feeling of camaraderie between soldiers continued after the war was over. Sassoon spoke for many when he wrote that 'the man who really endured the War at its worst was everlastingly differentiated from everyone but his fellow soldiers' – a sentiment that pervades the poems in the last section AFTERMATH.[113] But the comradeship that had sustained them during the war often incapacitated them in the years that followed. Charles Carrington recalled: 'The 1916 fixation had caught me and stunted my mental growth, so that even ten years later I was retarded and adolescent. I could not escape from the comradeship of the trenches which had become a mental internment camp, or should I say a soldiers' home. I might as well have been in Chelsea Hospital.'[114] Some, like Ivor Gurney, never recovered: haunted by the camaraderie of the trenches and those 'lovely lost unhappy days', he moved inexorably towards madness and died in 1937 in a mental asylum.[115] Others, like Edgell Rickword in 'War and peace', aware of the fate of men like Gurney, turned their attention to strategies for survival. Many heterosexual men remembered their comrades with an affection that they were unlikely ever to feel again for another man. Edmund Blunden wondered ten years after the war had ended: 'Daniels, Davey, Ashford, Worley, Clifford, Seall, Unstead, do you remember me yet? I should know you among ten thousand. Your voices are heard, and each man longed for, beyond the maze of mutability.'[116] For homosexual men the situation was often more tragic. During the war Sassoon had written in his diary:

> When the war ends I'll be at the crossroads; and I know the path to choose. I must go out into the night alone. No fat settling down; the Hamner engagement was a ghastly blunder – It wouldn't work at all. That charming girl who writes to me so often would never be happy with me. It was my love for Bobbie [her brother] that led me to that mistake.[117]

But after the war, the reality of his erotic relationships could not compare with the chaste but passionate relationships he had enjoyed in the extraordinary circumstances of war. He wrote in 1920 during his affair with Gabriel Atkin:

> As I sit here, with some Elgar music in my head, I pull out my war-notebooks, and turn up June 30th 1916. Five years ago. It was the night before the Somme attack started. 'Last night' I was 'out cutting our wire from 12 till 3.30. Driven in once by shelling. Gibson's face in the first grey of dawn when he found me alone at wire-cutting.' . . . Gibson is a ghost, but he is more real to-night than

> the pianist who played Scriabin with such delicate adroitness. I wish I could 'find a moral equivalent for war'. To-night I feel as if I were only half-alive. Part of me died with all the Gibsons I used to know. Their memory makes Gabriel taste like a cheap liqueur.[118]

Sassoon's most important homosexual relationship in the post-war years was with Stephen Tennant, who must have at least made Gabriel Atkin seem like a fine wine. Unable to 'find a moral equivalent for war', Sassoon married in December 1933 and began his long journey towards the Catholic church.

J. B. Priestley decided that: 'There are those . . . who found in the war, however much thay hated it, the deeper reality we all look for . . . And almost all these men . . . seemed to feel confused and unhappy as the war receded, as if they were drifting away from reality, as if a world with its guns silent was an uneasy dream."[119] It was with this fear in mind that Robert Graves wrote to Wilfred Owen in December 1917: 'For God's sake cheer up and write more optimistically – the war's not over yet but a poet should have a spirit above wars.'[120] 'The deeper reality' sought by Priestley, and 'a spirit above wars' required by Graves, are common qualities shared by the poems in this anthology. While pertaining to a particular environment, these expressions of affection have a universality that goes beyond their immediate context, and which lends support to Charles Carrington's claim that: 'In its moral aspect, war resembles other great tragedies: the greater the horror, the nobler the triumph of the man who is not ruined by it.'[121] The vision of men creating human relationships in a destructive and meaningless world is of universal significance, but it would be a powerless vision were it not also an intimate one, and against Carrington's larger claims we should remember Richard Fein's observation that 'War poetry has the subversive tendency to be our age's love poetry.'[122]

This anthology testifies to the flowering of an extraordinary emotion, conceived and sustained in the most unlikely of circumstances; and although the dichotomy has to be accepted between the uniqueness of the theme and the variable quality of much of the verse, the power of the poems is undeniable, and the spectacle of men trying to manage almost unmanageable emotions a moving one. Though we may not have lived through the nightmares of the Western Front, we now have nightmares of our own, and these fragments of love, compassion, courage and endurance from another time and place still have a relevance for us today.

PRELUDE

AS TOILSOME I WANDERED VIRGINIA'S WOODS

As toilsome I wandered Virginia's woods,
To the music of rustling leaves kicked by my feet (For 'twas autumn),
I marked at the foot of a tree the grave of a soldier;
Mortally wounded he and buried on the retreat (easily all could I understand),
The halt of a midday hour, when up! no time to lose—yet this sign left,
On a tablet scrawled and nailed on the tree by the grave,
Bold, cautious, true, and my loving comrade.

Long, long I muse, then on my way go wandering,
Many a changeful season to follow, and many a scene of life,
Yet at times through changeful season and scene, abrupt, alone, or in the crowded street,
Comes before me the unknown soldier's grave, comes the inscription rude in Virginia's woods,
Bold, cautious, true, and my loving comrade.

WALT WHITMAN

THE CALL

I remember well the face of a kind, keen major . . . amid a crowded room at the War Office. He smiled at each of us in turn, but his eyes were sad. 'How old are you?' he asked an applicant who was blowing out a bare chest to fill the tape around it. 'Nineteen, sir.' 'You seem in a great hurry to be killed, my boy.' The applicant, disconcerted, stammered, 'I only want to do my bit, sir.' 'Very well, so you shall, so you shall; and good luck to you.' But, you know, as the major laid his head against my bare chest – I was next – I experienced a strange sensation: his eye-lashes were wet.

ROBERT NICHOLS[123]

GLIMPSE

I saw you fooling often in the tents
With fair dishevelled hair and laughing lips,
And frolic elf lights in your careless eyes,
As who had never known the taste of tears
Or the world's sorrow. Then on march one night,
Halted beneath the stars I heard the sound
Of talk and laughter, and glanced back to see
If you were there. But you stood far apart
And silent, bowed upon your rifle butt,
And gazed into the night as one who sees.
I marked the drooping lips and fathomless eyes
And knew you brooded on immortal things.

O.T.C. *Camp, June* 1914

W. N. HODGSON

THE SUN USED TO SHINE

The sun used to shine while we two walked
Slowly together, paused and started
Again, and sometimes mused, sometimes talked
As either pleased, and cheerfully parted

Each night. We never disagreed
Which gate to rest on. The to be
And the late past we gave small heed.
We turned from men or poetry

To rumours of the war remote
Only till both stood disinclined
For aught but the yellow flavorous coat
Of an apple wasps had undermined;

Or a sentry of dark betonies,
The stateliest of small flowers on earth,
At the forest verge; or crocuses
Pale purple as if they had their birth

In sunless Hades fields. The war
Came back to mind with the moonrise
Which soldiers in the east afar
Beheld then. Nevertheless, our eyes

Could as well imagine the Crusades
Or Caesar's battles. Everything
To faintness like those rumours fades—
Like the brook's water glittering

Under the moonlight—like those walks
Now—like us two that took them, and
The fallen apples, all the talks
And silences—like memory's sand

When the tide covers it late or soon,
And other men through other flowers
In those fields under the same moon
Go talking and have easy hours.

EDWARD THOMAS

DEDICATION

To W.D.G., J.C.B., and other young soldiers

We have heard the bees and felt the sun grow hot on the face
together,
And watched the great clouds tumbling up across the Sussex down;
We found the same clouds farther north and the bees among the
heather,

Where the woods are old and silent and the pools are dark and
brown.

We've read and laughed and played, good Lord! and talked the slow
sun under,
And heard the nightjars whirring and the rooks go home to bed,
And watched the harvest moon come up, a white and shining wonder,
And all the bright star-companies go marching overhead.

The sweetest hour of all sweet hours is the hour when, long
unbroken,
A comfort and a silence fall that do not ask for speech;
The finest word of all fine words is the word that stays unspoken,
But rests with both a crystal thought no utterance can reach.

God grant, dear lad, that once again we walk the moors together,
And greet the sun and feel the wind blow fresh on face and lips,
Or stretch and dream upon the down in golden summer weather,
And watch our thoughts flock from us like the swift white wings of
ships.

J. L. CROMMELIN BROWN

BITTER-FRESH

Goes a boy fresh-singing
In the hill-trapt dale,
As the lark's heart in him springing
Highest Heaven would scale.

How can you be singing
Oh! so bitter-fresh,
Whom the murderous net and clinging
Tightens to enmesh?

Let be, lad, your singing;
O lad, let it be!
For the lark in you is wringing
The man's heart in me.

But lark and you go singing
To clouds big with thunder.
Bitter-fresh your song is, bringing
Me to weep and wonder.

GEOFFREY FABER

PEACE

Now, God be thanked Who has matched us with His hour,
And caught our youth, and wakened us from sleeping,
With hand made sure, clear eye, and sharpened power,
To turn, as swimmers into cleanness leaping,
Glad from a world grown old and cold and weary,
Leave the sick hearts that honour could not move,
And half-men, and their dirty songs and dreary,
And all the little emptiness of love!

Oh! we, who have known shame, we have found release there,
Where there's no ill, no grief, but sleep has mending,
Naught broken save this body, lost but breath;
Nothing to shake the laughing heart's long peace there
But only agony, and that has ending;
And the worst friend and enemy is but Death.

RUPERT BROOKE

BETTER FAR TO PASS AWAY

Better far to pass away
  While the limbs are strong and young,
Ere the ending of the day,
  Ere Youth's lusty song be sung.
Hot blood pulsing through the veins,
  Youth's high hope a burning fire,
Young men needs must break the chains
  That hold them from their heart's desire.

My friends the hills, the sea, the sun,
  The winds, the woods, the clouds, the trees—
How feebly, if my youth were done,
  Could I, an old man, relish these!
With laughter, then, I'll go to greet
  What Fate has still in store for me,
And welcome Death if we should meet,
  And bear him willing company.

My share of fourscore years and ten
  I'll gladly yield to any man,
And take no thought of 'where' or 'when,'
  Contented with my shorter span.
For I have learned what love may be,
  And found a heart that understands,
And known a comrade's constancy,
  And felt the grip of friendly hands.

Come when it may, the stern decree
  For me to leave the cheery throng
  And quit the sturdy company
    Of brothers that I work among.
  No need for me to look askance,
    Since no regret my prospect mars.
  My day was happy – and perchance
    The coming night is full of stars.

RICHARD DENNYS

WHEN THE DUST AND TOIL ARE OVER

When the dust and toil are over,
And the harsh broad glare of day
Fades to evening, when the longing
And the love have died away,

Somewhere in a moonbeam garden
Where the light is soft and blue,
'Neath the grass and silver shadow
I shall lie and dream of you.

There for ever and for ever
Undisturbèd I shall be:
In the everlasting silence,
'Neath the shadow of the tree.

'REX' FRESTON

TO MY FRIEND
(With an identity disc)

If ever I had dreamed of my dead name
High in the heart of London, unsurpassed
By Time for ever, and the Fugitive, Fame,
There taking a long sanctuary at last,—

Or if I onetime hope to hide its shame
—Shame of success, and sorrow of defeats,—
Under those holy cypresses, the same
That keep in shade the quiet place of Keats.

Now rather thank I God there is no risk
Of gravers scoring it with florid screed,
But let my death be memoried on this disc.
Wear it, sweet friend. Inscribe no date nor deed.
But may thy heart-beat kiss it, night and day,
Until the name grow blurred and wear away.

WILFRED OWEN

IF I SHOULD DIE, BE NOT CONCERNED TO KNOW

If I should die, be not concerned to know
  The manner of my ending, if I fell
Leading a folorn charge against the foe,
  Strangled by gas, or shattered by a shell.
Nor seek to see me in this death-in-life
  Mid shirks and curses, oaths and blood and sweat,
Cold in the darkness, on the edge of strife,
  Bored and afraid, irresolute, and wet.

But if you think of me, remember one
  Who loved good dinners, curious parody,
Swimming, and lying naked in the sun,
  Latin hexameters, and heraldry,
Athenian subtleties of δηζ and ποιζ,
  Beethoven, Botticelli, beer, and boys.

PHILIP BAINBRIGGE

THE MODERN ACHILLES

The linked smooth muscles round his form,
 The ripe blood blooms in his face;
The dark hair-clusters swarm
 About his forehead. Grace
Is his, and strength, and virile loveliness
Of limb, and cool address.

There is blue fire playing fierce
 In the broad-irised eyes.
His glances swoop and pierce
 And stay not in surmise,
But hovering, like the sparrow-hawk they hover
The helpless doomed prey over.

Loving or hating, his action is a king's.
 He brooks no weak reply.
In him the blood-stream sings,
 The full-fledged passions cry.
It is no ease to lie in his arms' clasp
Or to endure his grasp.

All the fine arguments that wise men weave
 And all the fine-spun art
Of song or picture leave
 Unwrung, unstirred, his heart;
He pictures only his desires as ends
And cares not how he spends.

O glorious, o handsome, o admired
 Prince and pattern of men,
Envied, mimicked, desired,
 Whom out of every ten
Nine do confess and take as man's ideal,
The strong, the brave, the real!

How fares it with you when the eternal test
Is held, at word of him
To whom meek hearts are best,
To whom the headstrong whim
That overbears your fellows is but the wild
Weak humour of a child?

How fares it then? What else have you to show?
What sacrifice of strength
That others' lives might go
Unsullied all their length,
What clearing in the forest of your mind
For God or human kind?

GEOFFREY FABER

JOINING-UP

No, not for you the glamour of emprise,
Poor driven lad with terror in your eyes.

No dream of wounds and medals and renown
Called you like Love from your drab Northern town.

No haunting fife, dizzily shrill and sweet,
Came lilting drunkenly down your dingy street.

You will not change, with a swift catch of pride,
In the cold hut among the leers and oaths,
Out of your suit of frayed civilian clothes,
Into the blaze of khaki they provide.

Like a trapped animal you crouch and choke
In the packed carriage where the veterans smoke
And tell such pitiless tales of Over There,
They stop your heart dead short and freeze your hair.

Your body's like a flower on a snapt stalk,
Your head hangs from your neck as blank as chalk.

What horrors haunt you, head upon your breast!
. . . O but you'll die as bravely as the rest!

LOUIS GOLDING

IN BARRACKS

The Barrack-square, washed clean with rain,
Shines wet and wintry-grey and cold.
Young Fusiliers, strong-legged and bold,
March and wheel and march again.
The sun looks over the barrack gate,
Warm and white with glaring shine,
To watch the soldiers of the Line
That life has hired to fight with fate.

Fall out: the long parades are done.
Up comes the dark; down goes the sun.
The square is walled with windowed light.
Sleep well, you lusty Fusiliers;
Shut your brave eyes on sense and sight,
And banish from your dreamless ears
The bugle's dying notes that say,
'Another night; another day.'

SIEGFRIED SASSOON

THE HALT

'Mark time in front! Rear fours cover! Company—halt!
Order arms! Stand at—ease! Stand easy.' A sudden hush:
And then the talk began with a mighty rush—
'You weren't ever in step—The sergeant—It wasn't my fault—

Well, the Lord be praised at least for a ten minutes' halt.'
 We sat on a gate and watched them easing and shifting;
 Out of the distance a faint, keen breath came drifting,
From the sea behind the hills, and the hedges were salt.

Where do you halt now? Under what hedge do you lie?
 Where the tall poplars are fringing the white French roads?
And smoke I have not seen discolours the foreign sky?
Is the company resting there as we rested together
 Stamping its feet and readjusting its loads
And looking with wary eyes at the drooping weather?

EDWARD SHANKS

THE NIGHT YOU WENT

(from the sonnet sequence 'Specimen of Agony V')

The night you went, I remember how your friends
Shouted and you gave back jest for gay jest,
But I stood silent by. As a sapling bends
To wind, so I bent dumb to sorrow, lest
Saying one word more I should break, betray
That bond between us whereof none else knew.
So I stood silent, till you drove away
Into the night. But, as you went from view,
I turned and in my own room and alone
Surrendered to the grief which has no name
Unless despair, no utterance but a groan,
No form except the black void of love's flame;
And almost prayed that I had never seen
Your face or that our love had never been.

GEOFFREY FABER

TO RUPERT BROOKE

He's gone.
I do not understand.
I only know
That as he turned to go
And waved his hand
In his young eyes a sudden glory shone:
And I was dazzled by a sunset glow,
And he was gone.

WILFRED GIBSON

FRAGMENT

I strayed about the deck, an hour, to-night
Under a cloudy moonless sky; and peeped
In at the windows, watched my friends at table,
Or playing cards, or standing in the doorway,
Or coming out into the darkness. Still
No one could see me.

I would have thought of them
—Heedless, within a week of battle—in pity,
Pride in their strength and in the weight and firmness
And link'd beauty of bodies, and pity that
This gay machine of splendour 'ld soon be broken,
Thought little of, pashed, scattered . . .
Only, always,
I could but see them—against the lamplight—pass
Like coloured shadows, thinner than filmy glass,
Slight bubbles, fainter than the wave's faint light,
That broke to phosphorus out in the night,
Perishing things and strange ghosts—soon to die
To other ghosts—this one, or that, or I.

RUPERT BROOKE

SOMEWHERE IN FRANCE

Here I am in a signal dugout with some of the nicest, and most handsome young men I ever met. And would you believe it? – my luck I mean; they talk their native language and sing their own folksongs with sweet natural voices. I did not sleep at all for the first day in the dugout – there was too much to be said, asked, and experienced: and pleasure in watching their quick expressions for oblivion. It was one of the notable evenings of my life.

IVOR GURNEY[124]

PALS O' MINE

Morning came—
Out of its golden mist I heard
Laughter and the echoed tramp
Of a thousand laughing lads.
Over the hill, with measured tread
They came . . . each young heart fired
With a myriad gleaming hopes.
The morning sun
Made all the world seem warm and glad.
They passed along—a khaki throng
With a smile and a jest, and I heard the song
Of those dear laughing lads.

Came noontide—
A solemn peace around me fell.
Laughter and happy song
Grew silent, the measured tread
Of that splendid throng died softly away—
Like the ending of a day . . . somehow I felt
The empty loneliness of a world grown cold.
. . . Then evening came.
Behind the lonely hill
The sun sank crimson . . . through the trees
The night wind softly stirred
And all was still.
. . . But I shall hear
When morning comes in a golden mist,
The echoed song from the thousand lips
Of those dear laughing lads.

RAYMOND HEYWOOD

FIRST TIME IN

After the dread tales and red yarns of the Line
Anything might have come to us; but the divine
Afterglow brought us up to a Welsh colony
Hiding in sandbag ditches, whispering consolatory
Soft foreign things. Then we were taken in
To low huts candle-lit, shaded close by slitten
Oilsheets, and there the boys gave us kind welcome,
So that we looked out as from the edge of home,
Sang us Welsh things, and changed all former notions
To human hopeful things. And the next day's guns
Nor any line-pangs ever quite could blot out
The strangely beautiful entry to war's rout;
Candles they gave us, precious and shared over-rations—
Ulysses found little more in his wanderings without doubt.
'David of the White Rock', the 'Slumber Song' so soft, and that
Beautiful tune to which roguish words by Welsh pit boys
Are sung—but never more beautiful than there under the guns'
noise.

IVOR GURNEY

From 'IN PARENTHESIS, PART 7'

Riders on pale horses loosed
and vials irreparably broken
an' Wat price bleedin' Glory
Glory
Glory Hallelujah
and the Royal Welsh sing:
Jesu
lover of me soul . . . to *Aberystwyth*.
But that was on the right with
the genuine Taffies
but we are rash levied

from Islington and Hackney
and the purlieus of Walworth
flashers from Surbiton
men of the stock of Abraham
from Bromley-by-Bow
Anglo-Welsh from Queens Ferry
rosary-wallahs from Pembrey Dock
lighterman with a Norway darling
from Greenland Stairs
and two lovers from Ebury Bridge,
Bates and Coldpepper
that men called the Lily-white boys.
Fowler from Harrow and the House who'd lost his way into
this crush who was gotten in a parsonage on a maye.
Dynamite Dawes the old 'un
and Diamond Phelps his batty
from Santiago del Estero
and Bulawayo respectively,
both learned in ballistics
                and wasted on a line-mob.

DAVID JONES

PHOTOGRAPHS

(To two Scots lads)

Lying in dug-outs, joking idly, wearily;
    Watching the candle guttering in the draught;
Hearing the great shells go high over us, eerily
    Singing; how often have I turned over, and laughed

With pity and pride, photographs of all colours,
    All sizes, subjects: khaki brothers in France;
Or mothers' faces worn with countless dolours;
    Or girls whose eyes were challenging and must dance,

Though in a picture only, a common cheap
  Ill-taken card; and children—frozen, some
(Babies) waiting on Dicky-bird to peep
  Out of the handkerchief that is his home

(But he's so shy!). And some with bright looks, calling
  Delight across the miles of land and sea,
That not the dread of barrage suddenly falling
  Could quite blot out—not mud nor lethargy.

Smiles and triumphant careless laughter. O
  The pain of them, wide Earth's most sacred things!
Lying in dug-outs, hearing the great shells slow
  Sailing mile-high, the heart mounts higher and sings.

But once—O why did he keep that bitter token
  Of a dead Love?—that boy, who, suddenly moved,
Showed me, his eyes wet, his low talk broken,
  A girl who better had not been beloved.

IVOR GURNEY

SENTRY GO

True lad who shared the guard with me
That night of whirling snow,
What other nights have brought to you
I may not know.

Although I never heard your name,
And hardly saw your face,
You poured out all your heart to me
As we kept pace.

I don't know if you're living still
Or fallen in the fight;
But in my heart your heart is safe
Till the last night.

WILFRED GIBSON

MY COMPANY (i)

You became
In many acts and quiet observances
A body souled, entire . . .

I cannot tell
What time your life became mine;
Perhaps when one summer night
We halted on the roadside
In the starlight only,
And you sang your sad home-songs,
Dirges which I standing outside your soul
Coldly condemned.

Perhaps one night, descending cold,
When rum was mighty acceptable,
And my doling gave birth to sensual gratitude.

And then our fights: we've fought together
Compact, unanimous;
And I have felt the pride of leadership.

In many acts and quiet observances
You absorbed me;
Until one day I stood eminent
And saw you gathered round me,
Uplooking,
And about you a radiance that seemed to beat
With variant glow and to give
Grace to our unity.

But, God! I know that I'll stand
Someday in the loneliest wilderness,
Someday my heart will cry
For the soul that has been but that now
Is scattered with the winds,
Deceased and devoid.

I know that I'll wander with a cry:
'O beautiful men, O men I loved,
O whither are you gone, my company?'

This is a hell
Immortal while I live.

HERBERT READ

FOOT INSPECTION

The twilight barn was chinked with gleams; I saw
Soldiers with naked feet stretched on the straw,
Stiff-limbed from the long muddy march we'd done,
And ruddy-faced with April wind and sun.
With pity and stabbing tenderness I see
Those stupid, trustful eyes stare up at me.
Yet, while I stoop to Morgan's blistered toes
And ask about his boots, he never knows
How glad I'd be to die, if dying could set him free
From battles. Shyly grinning at my joke,
He pulls his grimy socks on; lights a smoke,
And thinks 'Our officer's a decent bloke'.

SIEGFRIED SASSOON

THE ESTAMINET

The crowd of us were drinking
One night at Riez Bailleul,
The glasses were a-clinking,
The estaminet was full;

And loud with song and story
And blue with tales and smoke,—
We spoke no word of glory,
Nor mentioned 'foreign yoke.'

But yarns of girls in Blighty;
Vain, jolly, ugly, fair,
Standoffish, foolish, flighty—
And O! that we were there!

Where never thuds a 'Minnie',
But Minnie smiles at you
A-meeting in the spinney,
With kisses not a few.

And of an inn that Johnson
Does keep; the 'Rising Sun'.
His friends him call Jack Johnson,
He's Gloster's only one.

And talk of poachers' habits
(But girls ever and again)
Of killing weasels, rabbits,
Stoats, pheasants, never men,

Although we knew to-morrow
Must take us to the line,
In beer hid thought and sorrow,
In ruddy and white wine.

When all had finished drinking,
  Though still was clear each head,
We said no word—went slinking
  Straight homeward (?), into bed (?).

O never lads were merrier,
  Nor straighter nor more fine,
Though we were only 'Terrier'
  And only, 'Second Line'.

O I may get to Blighty,
  Or hell, without a sign
Of all the love that filled me,
  Leave dumb the love that filled me,
The flood of love that filled me
  For these dear comrades of mine.

IVOR GURNEY

THE BATHE

Come friend and swim. We may be better then,
  But here the dust blows ever in the eyes
And wrangling round are weary fevered men,
    For ever mad with flies.
I cannot sleep, nor even long lie still,
  And you have read your April paper twice;
To-morrow we must stagger up the hill
    To man a trench and live among the lice.

But yonder, where the Indians have their goats,
  There is a rock stands sheer above the blue,
Where one may sit and count the bustling boats
    And breathe the cool air through;
May find it still is good to be alive,
  May look across and see the Trojan shore
Twinkling and warm, may strip, and stretch, and dive.—
    And for a space forget about the war.

Then will we sit and talk of happy things,
Home and 'the High' and some far fighting friend,
And gather strength for what the morrow brings,
For that may be the end.
It may be we shall never swim again,
Never be clean and comely to the sight,
May rot untombed and stink with all the slain.
Come, then, and swim. Come and be clean to-night.

A. P. HERBERT

THE BATTLEFIELD

Around no fire the soldiers sleep to-night,
But lie a-wearied on the ice-bound field,
With cloaks wrapt round their sleeping forms, to shield
Them from the northern winds. Ere comes the light
Of morn brave men must arm, stern foes to fight.
The sentry stands his limbs with cold congealed;
His head a-nod with sleep; he cannot yield,
Though sleep and snow in deadly force unite.

Amongst the sleepers lies the Boy awake,
And wide-eyed plans brave glories that transcend
The deeds of heroes dead; then dreams o'ertake
His tired-out brain, and lofty fancies blend
To one grand theme, and through all barriers break
To guard from hurt his faithful sleeping friend.

SYDNEY OSWALD

THE RETURN

There's a tramp o' feet in the mornin,'
There's an oath from an N.C.O.,
As up the road to the trenches
The brown battalions go:
Guns and rifles and wagons,
Transports and horses and men,
Up with the flush of the dawnin',
And back with the night again.

Back again from the battle,
From the mates we've left behind,
And our officers are gloomy
And the N.C.O.s are kind;
When a Jew's harp breaks the silence,
Purring an old refrain,
Singing the song of the soldier,
'Here we are again!'

Here we are!
Here we are!
Oh! here we are again!
Some have gone west,
Best of the best,
Lying out in the rain,
Stiff as stones in the open,
Out of the doings for good.
They'll never come back to advance or attack;
But, God! don't we wish that they could!

PATRICK MACGILL

PRELUDE: THE TROOPS

Dim, gradual thinning of the shapeless gloom
Shudders to drizzling daybreak that reveals
Disconsolate men who stamp their sodden boots
And turn dulled, sunken faces to the sky
Haggard and hopeless. They, who have beaten down
The stale despair of night, must now renew
Their desolation in the truce of dawn,
Murdering the livid hours that grope for peace.

Yet these who cling to life with stubborn hands,
Can grin through storm of death and find a gap
In the clawed, cruel tangles of his defence.
They march from safety, and the bird-sung joy
Of grass-green thickets, to the land where all
Is ruin, and nothing blossoms but the sky
That hastens over them where they endure
Sad, smoking, flat horizons, reeking woods,
And foundered trench-lines volleying doom for doom.

O my brave brown companions, when your souls
Flock silently away, and the eyeless dead
Shame the wild beast of battle on the ridge,
Death will stand grieving in that field of war
Since your unvanquished hardihood is spent.
And through some mooned Valhalla there will pass
Battalions and battalions, scarred from hell;
The unreturning army that was youth;
The legions who have suffered and are dust.

SIEGFRIED SASSOON

KILLED IN ACTION

. . . the boy by my side, shot through the head, lay on top of me, soaking my shoulder, for half an hour. Catalogue? Photograph? Can you photograph the crimson-hot iron as it cools from the smelting? That is what Jones's blood looked like, and felt like. My senses are charred.

WILFRED OWEN[125]

KISMET

Opal fires in the Western sky
  (For that which is written must ever be),
And a bullet comes droning, whining by,
  To the heart of a sentry close to me.

For some go early, and some go late
  (A dying scream on the evening air)
And who is there that believes in Fate
  As a soul goes out in the sunset flare?

R. B. MARRIOTT-WATSON

I SAW HIS ROUND MOUTH'S CRIMSON

I saw his round mouth's crimson deepen as it fell,
  Like a Sun, in his last deep hour;
Watched the magnificent recession of farewell,
  Clouding, half gleam, half glower,
And a last splendour burn the heavens of his cheek.
  And in his eyes
The cold stars lighting, very old and bleak,
  In different skies.

WILFRED OWEN

VICTORY

I watched it oozing quietly
  Out of the gaping gash.
The lads thrust on to victory
  With lunge and curse and crash.

Half-dazed, that uproar seemed to me
  Like some old battle-sound
Heard long ago, as quietly
  His blood soaked in the ground.

The lads thrust on to victory
  With lunge and crash and shout.
I lay and watched, as quietly
  His life was running out.

WILFRED GIBSON

From 'IN PARENTHESIS, PART 7'

But where's Fatty and Smiler—and this Watcyn boasts he'd
seen the open land beyond the trees, with Jerry coming on in mass—
and they've left Diamond between the beech boles
and old Dawes blaspheming quietly;
and there's John Hales with Wop Castello cross legged under
the sallies, preoccupied with dead lines—gibbering the formulae of
  their profession—
Wop defends the D III converted;

and Bates without Coldpepper
digs like a Bunyan muck-raker for his weight for woe.

DAVID JONES

THE FACE

Out of the smoke of men's wrath,
The red mist of anger,
Suddenly,
As a wraith of sleep,
A boy's face, white and tense,
Convulsed with terror and hate,
The lips trembling . . .

Then a red smear, falling . . .
I thrust aside the cloud, as it were tangible,
Blinded with a mist of blood.
The face cometh again
As a wraith of sleep:
A boy's face delicate and blonde,
The very mask of God,
Broken.

FREDERIC MANNING

From 'IN PARENTHESIS, PART 7'

The First Field Dressing is futile as frantic as seaman's shift
bunged to stoved bulwark, so soon the darking flood percolates
and he dies in your arms.
    And get back to that digging can't yer –
this ain't a bloody Wake
        for these dead, who will soon have their dead
for burial clods heaped over.
Nor time for halsing
nor to clip green wounds
nor weeping Maries bringing anointments
neither any word spoken
nor no decent nor appropriate sowing of this seed

nor remembrance of the harvesting
of the renascent cycle
and return
nor shaving of the head nor ritual incising for these *viriles*
under each tree
No one sings: Lully lully
for the mate whose blood runs down.

DAVID JONES

FUTILITY

Move him into the sun—
Gently its touch awoke him once,
At home, whispering of fields half-sown.
Always it woke him, even in France,
Until this morning and this snow.
If anything might rouse him now
The kind old sun will know.

Think how it wakes the seeds—
Woke once the clays of a cold star.
Are limbs, so dear achieved, are sides
Full-nerved, still warm, too hard to stir?
Was it for this the clay grew tall?
—O what made fatuous sunbeams toil
To break earth's sleep at all?

WILFRED OWEN

MY PAL

Just now he spoke to me—I heard his laughter,
He knew the joy of life like other men,
One moment after
I heard a moan—a muffled cry of pain
And then . . . and then I saw a crimson stain
Upon the moonlit space where I was kneeling;
A madness o'er me crept, my heart grew numb
And dead to every feeling.

Dear God, can I not stay
And share his cross?
Ah, no! I needs must turn away
Dry-eyed and silent, and from day to day
My heart shall mourn its loss.

Beneath the moon, grief pale, I clasp his hand,
And for a quiet while
I bend above him, and his tired smile
Will linger in my heart until the end . . .
O God! 'tis only they who loved a friend
Can understand!

RAYMOND HEYWOOD

A MAY MORNING

When morning came
I stood half dazed in that strange aftermath
Of men who cast a dice with Death
And win—
Yet see their fellow players lose.
Near me—a khaki heap,
And others everywhere.
A burning in my arm.
Another wound
That in fierce moments brought me agony.

I counted the crumpled heaps
And, finishing, began again
Tiredly wondering.
Then ceased to count
And thought.
Then could not think
So still must count and count.

My soul! I was so tired
And yet I stayed.
For the nearest heap
Was a boy who had watched me always
Having great trust in me,
Believing me strong.
And now
I could not let him see that I was weak.
For he lay so still
And I could feel even though I did not touch,
That his fingers were stiff and cold
Which I had clasped warm, last night—
Encouraging.
And I could see even when I did not look
Trust in his fixed eyes
Watching me still.

A. NEWBERRY CHOYCE

From 'THE SONG OF TIADATHA'

Had you been there when the dawn broke.
Had you looked from out the trenches,
You'd have seen that Serbian hillside,
Seen the aftermath of battle.
Seen the scattered picks and shovels,
Seen the scraps of stray equipment,
Here and there a lonely rifle,
Or a Lewis gun all twisted,
Seen the little heaps of khaki
Lying huddled on the hillside,
Huddled by the Bulgar trenches
Very still and very silent,
Nothing stirring, nothing moving,
Save a very gallant doctor
And his band of stretcher bearers,
Working fearless in the open,
Giving water to the dying,
Bringing in those broken soldiers.
You'd have seen the sunlight streaming,
And perhaps you would have wondered
How the sun could still be shining,
How the birds could still be singing,
While so many British soldiers
Lay so still upon the hillside.

OWEN RUTTER

SOLILOQUY I

I was wrong, quite wrong;
The dead men are not always carrion.
After the advance,
As we went through the shattered trenches
Which the enemy had left,
We found, lying upon the fire-step,
A dead English soldier,
His head bloodily bandaged
And his closed left hand touching the earth,

More beautiful than one can tell,
More subtly coloured than a perfect Goya,
And more austere and lovely in repose
Than Angelo's hand could ever carve in stone.

RICHARD ALDINGTON

MY COMPANY (iii)

A man of mine
lies on the wire.
It is death to fetch his soulless corpse.

A man of mine
lies on the wire;
And he will rot
And first his lips
The worms will eat.

It is not thus I would have him kissed,
But with the warm passionate lips
Of his comrade here.

HERBERT READ

CASUALTY

They are bringing him down.
He looks at me wanly.
The bandages are brown,
Brown with mud, red only—
But how deep a red!—in the breast of the shirt,
Deepening red, too, as each whistling breath
Is drawn with the suck of a slow-filling squirt,
While waxen cheeks waste to the pallor of death.

O my comrade,
My comrade, that you could rest
Your tired body on mine! That your head might be laid—
Fallen and heavy—upon this my breast!
That I might take your hands in my hands
To chafe! That, abandoned, your body might sink
Upon mine, which here helplessly, grievously stands;
That your body might drink
Warmth from my body, strength from my veins,
Life from my heart, that monstrously beats
After you vainly!
The trench curves. They are gone.

The steep rain teems down.

O my companion!
Who were you? How did you come
Looking so vainly upon me? I know—
And oh, how immensely long I have known—
Those aching eyes, numb face, gradual gloom,
That depth without groan!

Take now my love—this love which alone
I can give you—and shed without pain
That life, if I could, I would succour
With this the pulse of my own!

ROBERT NICHOLS

THE DEATH-BED

He drowsed and was aware of silence heaped
Round him, unshaken as the steadfast walls;
Aqueous like floating rays of amber light,
Soaring and quivering in the wings of sleep.
Silence and safety; and his mortal shore
Lipped by the inward, moonless waves of death.

Someone was holding water to his mouth.
He swallowed, unresisting; moaned and dropped
Through crimson gloom to darkness; and forgot
The opiate throb and ache that was his wound.
  Water—calm, sliding green above the weir.
  Water—a sky-lit alley for his boat,
  Bird-voiced, and bordered with reflected flowers
  And shaken hues of summer; drifting down,
  He dipped contented oars, and sighed, and slept.

Night, with a gust of wind, was in the ward,
Blowing the curtain to a glimmering curve.
Night. He was blind; he could not see the stars
Glinting among the wraiths of wandering cloud;
Queer blots of colour, purple, scarlet, green,
Flickered and faded in his drowning eyes.

Rain—he could hear it rustling through the dark;
Fragrance and passionless music woven as one;
Warm rain on drooping roses; pattering showers
That soak the woods; not the harsh rain that sweeps
Behind the thunder, but a trickling peace,
Gently and slowly washing life away.

He stirred, shifting his body; then the pain
Leapt like a prowling beast, and gripped and tore
His groping dreams with grinding claws and fangs.
  But someone was beside him; soon he lay
  Shuddering because that evil thing had passed.
  And death, who'd stepped toward him, paused and stared.

Light many lamps and gather round his bed.
Lend him your eyes, warm blood, and will to live.
Speak to him; rouse him; you may save him yet.
He's young; he hated War; how should he die
When cruel old campaigners win safe through?

But death replied: 'I choose him.' So he went,
And there was silence in the summer night;
Silence and safety; and the veils of sleep.
Then, far away, the thudding of the guns.

SIEGFRIED SASSOON

MARK ANDERSON

On the low table by the bed
Where it was set aside last night,
Beyond the bandaged lifeless head,
It glitters in the morning light;

And as the hours of watching pass,
I cannot sleep, I cannot think,
But only gaze upon the glass
Of water that he could not drink.

WILFRED GIBSON

THE BURIAL IN FLANDERS

(H. S. G., Ypres, 1916)

Through the light rain I think I see them going,
Through the light rain under the muffled skies;
Across the fields a stealthy wet wind wanders,
The mist bedews their tunics, dizzies their brains.

Shoulder-high, khaki shoulder by shoulder,
They bear my Boy upon his last journey.
Night is closing. The wind sighs, ebbs, and falters . . .
They totter dreaming, deem they see his face.

Even as Vikings of old their slaughtered leader
Upon their shoulders, so now bear they on
All that remains of Boy, my friend, their leader,
An officer who died for them under the dawn.

O that I were there that I might carry,
Might share that bitter load in grief, in pride! . . .
I see upon bronze faces love, submission,
And a dumb sorrow for that cheerful Boy.

Now they arrive. The priest repeats the service.
The drifting rain obscures.
They are dispersed.
The dying sun streams out: a moment's radiance;
The still, wet, glistening grave; the trod sward steaming.

* * *

Sudden great guns startle, echoing on the silence.
Thunder. Thunder.
HE HAS FALLEN IN BATTLE.
(O Boy! Boy!)
Lessening now. The rain
Patters anew. Far guns rumble and shudder
And night descends upon the desolate plain.

ROBERT NICHOLS

ASLEEP

Under his helmet, up against his pack,
After the many days of work and waking,
Sleep took him by the brow and laid him back.
And in the happy no-time of his sleeping,
Death took him by the heart. There was a quaking
Of the aborted life within him leaping . . .
Then chest and sleepy arms once more fell slack.
And soon the slow, stray blood came creeping
From the intrusive lead, like ants on track.

* * *

Whether his deeper sleep lie shaded by the shaking
Of great wings, and the thoughts that hung the stars,
High pillowed on calm pillows of God's making
Above these clouds, these rains, these sleets of lead,
And these winds' scimitars;
—Or whether yet his thin and sodden head
Confuses more and more with the low mould,
His hair being one with the grey grass
And finished fields of autumns that are old . . .
Who knows? Who hopes? Who troubles? Let it pass!
He sleeps. He sleeps less tremulous, less cold
Than we who must awake, and waking, say Alas!

WILFRED OWEN

MATES

Last night – O lucky me! – a Scottish Rifle sat up besides the stove with me, which glowed and made believe it was a fire. And he had travelled and could talk, and we had the same politics and the same tastes. His eyes were steady, his laugh open and easily provoked, and a smile that could not long be checked being chiefly an affair of the eyes. O well, it must have been 12.30 when we illicitly walked under the stars, watching Orion and hearing his huge sustained chord through the night.

IVOR GURNEY[126]

SOLDIERS

To R.A.

Brother,
I saw you on a muddy road
in France
pass by with your battalion,
rifle at the slope, full marching order,
arm swinging;
and I stood at ease,
folding my hands over my rifle,
with my battalion.
You passed me by, and our eyes met.
We had not seen each other since the days
we climbed the Devon hills together:
our eyes met, startled;
and, because the order was Silence,
we dared not speak.

O face of my friend,
alone distinct of all that company,
you went on, you went on,
into the darkness;
and I sit here at my table,
holding back my tears,
with my jaw set and my teeth clenched,
knowing I shall not be
even so near you as I saw you
in my dream.

F. S. FLINT

TWO NIGHTS

The moon's rim
Was over the wood,
As I trod with him
The quiet road.

The trees by the pond
Were still as stone;
The trees beyond
Were all alone.

Darkness clung
On the whole place;
A gleam swung
On the water's face.

And we talked of things
Of the dead days—
Forgotten stings,
Forgotten praise—

Till the sundered threads,
Were all bound,
And the old gods' heads
Were all crowned . . .

As a sudden star
Stabs the night,
There came afar
The burden light

Of some mean song—
Before I knew
I stood among
The men, with you.

The moon was high
Over us then;
Suddenly
One of the men

Started to sing
Low, very low,
That same thing
Had moved me so.

So for an hour
I stood at your side;
The moon was a still flower,
And the guns cried.

We did not speak much;
At the latter end
For a moment, the touch
Of a warm hand,

And the calm look
Of quiet eyes—
These things spoke . . .
(God! if he dies.)

I turned, and said,
'We'd better go;
(God! if he's dead)
Time hurries so.'

H. L. SIMPSON

OUTPOSTS

Sentry, sentry, what did you see
At gaze from your post beside Lone Tree?
A star-shell flared like a burning brand
But I saw no movement in No Man's Land.

Sentry, sentry, what did you hear
As the night-wind fluttered the grasses near?
I heard a rifle-shot on the flank,
And my mate slid down to the foot of the bank.

Sentry, sentry, what did you do,
And hadn't your mate a word for you?
I lifted his head and called his name.
His lips moved once, but no sound came.

Sentry, sentry, what did you say
As you watched alone till break of day?
I prayed the Lord that I'd fire straight
If I saw the man that killed my mate.

F. W. D. BENDALL

MATEY

Not comin' back to-night, matey,
And reliefs are comin' through,
We're all goin' out all right, matey,
Only we're leavin' you.
Gawd! it's a bloody sin, matey,
Now that we've finished the fight,
We go when reliefs come in, matey,
But you're stayin' 'ere to-night.

Over the top is cold, matey—
You lie on the field alone,
Didn't I love you of old, matey,
Dearer than the blood of my own.
You were my dearest chum, matey—
(Gawd! but your face is white)
But now, though reliefs 'ave come, matey,
I'm goin' alone to-night.

I'd sooner the bullet was mine, matey—
Goin' out on my own,
Leavin' you 'ere in the line, matey,
All by yourself, alone.
Chum o' mine and you're dead, matey,
And this is the way we part,
The bullet went through your head, matey,
But Gawd! it went through my 'eart.

PATRICK MACGILL

HIS MATE

There's a broken battered village
  Somewhere up behind the line,
There's a dug-out and a bunk there,
  That I used to say were mine.

I remember how I reached them,
  Dripping wet and all forlorn,
In the dim and dreary twilight
  Of a weeping summer dawn.

All that week I'd buried brothers,
  In one bitter battle slain,
In one grave I laid two hundred.
  God! What sorrow and what rain!

And that night I'd been in trenches,
  Seeking out the sodden dead,
And just dropping them in shell holes,
  With a service swiftly said.

For the bullets rattled round me,
  But I couldn't leave them there,
Water-soaked in flooded shell holes,
  Reft of common Christian prayer.

So I crawled round on my belly,
  And I listened to the roar
Of the guns that hammered Thiepval,
  Like big breakers on the shore.

Then there spoke a dripping sergeant,
  When the time was growing late,
'Would you please to bury this one,
  'Cause 'e used to be my mate?'

So we groped our way in darkness
  To a body lying there,
Just a blacker lump of blackness,
  With a red blotch on his hair.

Though we turned him gently over,
  Yet I still can hear the thud,
As the body fell face forward,
  And then settled in the mud.

We went down upon our faces,
  And I said the service through,
From 'I am the Resurrection'
  To the last, the great 'adieu'.

We stood up to give the Blessing,
  And commend him to the Lord,
When a sudden light shot soaring
  Silver swift and like a sword.

At a stroke it slew the darkness,
Flashed its glory on the mud,
And I saw the sergeant staring
At a crimson clot of blood.

There are many kinds of sorrow
In this world of Love and Hate,
But there is no sterner sorrow
Than a soldier's for his mate.

G. A. STUDDERT KENNEDY

REQUIEM

Pour out your light, O stars, and do not hold
Your loveliest shining from earth's outworn shell—
Pure and cold your radiance, pure and cold
My dead friend's face as well.

IVOR GURNEY

TRENCH POETS

I knew a man, he was my chum,
but he grew blacker every day,
and would not brush the flies away,
nor blanch however fierce the hum
of passing shells; I used to read,
to rouse him, random things from Donne—
like 'Get with child a mandrake-root'.
But you can tell he was far gone,
for he lay gaping, mackerel-eyed,
and stiff and senseless as a post
even when that old poet cried
'I long to talk with some old lover's ghost.'

I tried the Elegies one day,
but he, because he heard me say:
'What needst thou have more covering than a man?'
grinned nastily, and so I knew
the worms had got his brains at last.
There was one thing that I might do
To starve the worms; I racked my head
for healthy things and quoted *Maud*.
His grin got worse and I could see
he sneered at passion's purity.
He stank so badly, though we were great chums
I had to leave him; then rats ate his thumbs.

EDGELL RICKWORD

From 'The Song of Tiadatha'

For a while my Tiadatha
Rested on the slopes of Hortiach,
Rested till he'd got his strength back.
Then at Summer Hill he sojourned,
Barren camp where no one lingers
Any longer than he's got to;
Thence he went by easy stages
Back to join the Royal Dudshires,
Found them up at Karasouli,
Found so many faces missing
That at first his heart was lonely,
But a few were still remaining,
Still a few familiar faces,
And they made him very welcome,
With them Woggs his soldier servant.
But although he made new comrades,
Carried on without the old ones,
Yet his heart was often lonely,
Lonely for those missing faces.

OWEN RUTTER

IN MEMORIAM

R. M. Stalker. Missing, September 1916

As I go down the highway,
  And through the village street,
I hear the pipers playing
  And the tramp of marching feet.
The men I worked and fought with
  Swing by me four on four,
And at the end you follow
  Whom I shall see no more.

Oh, Stalk, where are you lying?
  Somewhere and far away,
Enemy hands have buried
  Your quiet contemptuous clay.
There was no greeting given,
  No tear of friend for friend,
From us when you flew over
  Exultant to the end.

I couldn't see the paper,
  I couldn't think that you
Would never walk the highway
  The way you used to do.
I turn at every footfall,
  Half-hoping, half-afraid
To see you coming, later
  Than usual for parade.

The old Lairg clique is broken,
  I drove there yesterday,
And the car was full of ghosts that sat
  Beside me all the way.
Ghosts of old songs and laughter,
  Ghosts of the jolly three,
That went the road together
  And go no more with me.

Oh, Stalk, but I am lonely,
For the old days we knew,
And the bed on the floor at Lesdos
We slept in, I and you.
The joyful nights in billets
We laughed and drank and swore—
But the candle's burned out now, Stalk,
In the mess at Henancourt.

The candle's burned out now, old man,
And the dawn's come grey and cold,
And I sit by the fire here
Alone and sad and old.
Though all the rest come back again,
You lie in a foreign land,
And the strongest link of all the chain
Is broken in my hand.

E. A. MACKINTOSH

THE MESS TABLE

Sometimes, above the talk and wine
That round the long white table flow,
There fall upon my startled ears,
The voices that I used to know.

And looking round the lighted room,
Each in his own familiar chair,
With laughing eyes that greet my eyes,
I see the dead men sitting there.

The dead men's faces glow and shine
With jest and laughter as of old:
The dead men's voices come and go;
And yet my heart is strangely cold.

For one long moment they remain:
And then, as through a mist, I see
The new men sitting in the chairs,
Where once the dead men used to be.

'REX' FRESTON

I TRACKED A DEAD MAN

I tracked a dead man down a trench,
I knew not he was dead.
They told me he had gone that way,
And there his foot-marks led.

The trench was long and close and curved,
It seemed without an end;
And as I threaded each new bay
I thought to see my friend.

I went there stooping to the ground.
For, should I raise my head,
Death watched to spring; and how should then
A dead man find the dead?

At last I saw his back. He crouched
As still as still could be,
And when I called his name aloud
He did not answer me.

The floor-way of the trench was wet
Where he was crouching dead:
The water of the pool was brown,
And round him it was red.

I stole up softly where he stayed
  With head hung down all slack,
And on his shoulders laid my hands
  And drew him gently back.

And then, as I had guessed, I saw
  His head, and how the crown—
I saw then why he crouched so still,
  And why his head hung down.

W. S. S. LYON

HOW RIFLEMAN BROWN CAME TO VALHALLA

To the lower Hall of Valhalla, to the heroes of no renown,
Relieved from his spell at the listening-post, came Rifleman Joseph
  Brown.
With never a rent in his khaki nor smear of blood on his face,
He flung his pack from his shoulders, and made for an empty place.

The Killer-men of Valhalla looked up from the banquet-board
At the unfouled breech of his rifle, at the unfleshed point of his
  sword;
And the unsung dead of the trenches, the kings who have never a
  crown,
Demanded his pass to Valhalla from Rifleman Joseph Brown.

'*Who comes, unhit, to the party?*' A one-legged Corporal spoke,
And the gashed heads nodded approval through the rings of the
  Endless Smoke:
'*Who comes for the beer and the Woodbines of the never-closed Canteen,*
'*With the barrack-shine on his bayonet and a full-charged magazine?*'

Then Rifleman Brown looked round him at the nameless men of the
  Line—

At the wounds of the shell and the bullet, at the burns of the bomb
 and the mine;
At the tunics, virgin of medals but crimson-clotted with blood;
At the ankle-boots and the puttees, caked stiff with the Flanders mud;
At the myriad short Lee-Enfields that crowded the rifle-rack,
Each with its blade to the sword-boss brown, and its muzzle
 powder-black:

And Rifleman Brown said never a word; yet he felt in the soul of his
 soul
His right to the beer of the lower Hall, though he came to drink of it,
 whole;
His right to the fags of the free Canteen, to a seat at the
 banquet-board,
Though he came to the men who had killed their man, with never a
 man to his sword.

'Who speaks for the stranger Rifleman, O boys of the free Canteen?
Who passes the chap with the unmaimed limbs and the kit that is far too
 clean?'
The gashed heads eyed him above their beers, the gashed lips sucked
 at their smoke:
There were three at the board of his own platoon, but not a man of
 them spoke.

His mouth was mad for the tankard froth and the biting whiff of a fag,
But he knew that he might not speak for himself to the dead men who
 do not brag.

A gun-butt crashed on the gateway, a man came staggering in;
His head was cleft with a great red wound from the temple-bone to
 the chin,
His blade was dyed to the bayonet-boss with the clots that were
 scarcely dry;
And he cried to the men who had killed their man:
 'Who passes the Rifleman? I!
By the four I slew, by the shell I stopped, if my feet be not too late,

I speak the word for Rifleman Brown that a chap may speak for his
mate.'

The dead of lower Valhalla, the heroes of dumb renown,
They pricked their ears to a tale of the earth as they set their tankards
down.

'My mate was on sentry this evening when the General happened
along,
And asked what he'd do in a gas-attack, Joe told him: "Beat on the
gong."
"What else?"
"Open fire, Sir," Joe answered.
"Good God, man," our General said,
"By the time you'd beaten that bloodstained gong the chances are
you'd be dead.
Just think, lad." "Gas helmet, of course, Sir." "Yes, damn it, and *gas
helmet first.*"
So Joe stood dumb to attention, and wondered why he'd been
cursed.'

The gashed heads turned to the Rifleman, and now it seemed that
they knew
Why the face that had never a smear of blood was stained to the
jawbones, blue.

'He was posted again at midnight.' The scarred heads craned to the
voice,
As the man with the blood-red bayonet spoke up for the mate of his
choice.
'You know what it's like in a listening-post, the Véry candles aflare,
Their bullets smacking the sand-bags, our Vickers combing your hair,
How your ears and your eyes get jumpy, till each known tuft that you
scan
Moves and crawls in the shadows till you'd almost swear it was man;
You know how you peer and snuff at the night when the North-East
gas-winds blow.'

'*By the One who made us and maimed us*,' quoth lower Valhalla, '*we know!*'

'Sudden, out of the blackness, sudden as Hell, there came
Roar and rattle of rifles, spurts of machine-gun flame;
And Joe stood up in the forward sap to try and fathom the game.
Sudden, their shells come screaming; sudden, his nostrils sniff
The sickening reek of the rotten pears, the death that kills with a whiff.
Death! and he knows it certain, as he bangs on his cartridge-case,
With the gas-cloud's claws at his windpipe and the gas cloud's wings on his face . . .
We heard his gong in our dug-out, he only whacked on it twice,
We whipped our gas-bags over our heads, and manned the step in a trice—
For the cloud would have caught us as sure as Fate if he'd taken the Staff's advice.'

His head was cleft with a great red wound from the chin to the temple-bone,
But his voice was as clear as a sounding gong, 'I'll be damned if I'll drink alone,
Not even in lower Valhalla! Is he free of your free Canteen,
My mate who comes with the unfleshed point and the full-charged magazine?'

The gashed heads rose at the Rifleman o'er the rings of the Endless Smoke,
And loud as the roar of a thousand guns Valhalla's answer broke,
And loud as the crash of a thousand shells their tankards clashed on the board:
'He is free of the mess of the Killer-men, your mate of the unfleshed sword;
For we know the worth of his deed on earth: as we know the speed of the death
Which catches its man by the back of the throat and gives him water for breath;
As we know how the hand at the helmet-cloth may tarry seconds too long,

When the very life of the front-line trench is staked on the beat of a gong.
By the four you slew, by the case he smote, by the grey gas-cloud and the green,
We pass your mate for the Endless Smoke and the beer of the free Canteen.'

In the lower hall of Valhalla, with the heroes of no renown,
With our nameless dead of the Marne and the Aisne, of Mons, and of Wipers town,
With the men who killed ere they died for us, sits Rifleman Joseph Brown.

GILBERT FRANKAU

TO MY MATE

Old comrade, are you living, do you hear me, can you see,
If they print this stuff in Blighty, will you guess it comes from me?
I was just a wee bit balmy, don't you reckon, all the while?
And perhaps the life in Flanders didn't help to fix that tile;
As the R.S.M. expressed it, 'Who's the freak in Number Nine
Who looks as if his wits were umpteen kilos from the Line?'
So the Regimental copped it at the Cambrai do, I hear,
And the 'freak' is safe in 'civvies', with a pension like a peer;
And for all his dud deportment and the Regimental's scorn
He could work his blooming ticket with the smartest soldier born.

I never wrote, I own it, and I've not so much as tried
To find if you're in England yet, or on the other side;
But I never knew your number, and I lost your home address
With my pack and all inside it when I clicked for C.C.S.

But I haven't quite forgot you, and my only souvenir
That I wouldn't sell for sixpence is the thought of you, old dear.
We were mates to some good purpose in a world of boundless bad,
And to scheme each other's welfare was the one good thing we had.
We were some queer brace of partners: Fate was surely on the spree
When she yoked in double harness such a pair as you and me.

You'd a craze for searching corpses: I could never stand the smell.
You'd a deep respect for Scripture, and for words you couldn't spell.
You were gentler than a woman when you dressed a wounded limb;
And at grab—an old cat-mother is not half so quick and slim.
I think I see you sitting in our dug-out at Bapaume
Where you found your German wrist-watch (Did you ever get that home?)
With a sandbag on your napper, and your feet inside a pair,
While I punched a tin of Nestle's you had raised from God knows where.
I can see you sternly frowning, with my glasses on your nose,
While you proved from Revelations when the War was bound to close;
Till you smelt the old pot cooking, then your brow relaxed its frown
And you sat and purred with pleasure as you spooned the custard down.
Well, it's over now and ended; we shall never file again
Down the slimy, sodden mule-track in the darkness and the rain.
You would always come behind me on the duckboards if you could
To help me if I stumbled with my load of wire or wood.
I can hear you through the darkness, when you saw that I was done,
'There's a tin of strawberry pozzy in my pack: step up, old son!'

I've got the same old billet, in the same old office chair,
And France seems just as wild a dream as Blighty seemed out there.
But I don't get on with civvies; they know too much for me.
They've read the war news twice a day, not once a month like we.
They'll swallow bags of bunkum and let it down like pie,
But they think you daft or shell-shocked if you speak what aint a lie.
They love you if you spruce 'em well and give 'em lots of buck
Of the Prussian Guards you've strangled and the squealing Huns you've stuck.
They arn't half sweet on bayonet scraps and blood and all that tosh,
And they'd earn a D.C. medal-mint at shouting down the Bosche.
But they've never heard the rat-tat of the gun that can't be seen;
They've never watched the sheaves go down, and walked behind to glean;
They've made their 'Great Advances' with pins on paper maps;

They've done their 'Splendid Pushes' with a pusher on their laps.—
But it aint worth while to tell 'em: you might talk till all was blue,
But you'd never make 'em compree what a bloke out there goes
  through.

GEORGE WILLIS

MEMORIES

The tall pines tower gauntly
  Above my bedroom eaves,
With the moon, like a ghost, behind them,
  Peering between their leaves.
The air is warm and balmy,
  And the hillside bathed in light,
But a restless mood is on me
  As I think of another night.
Still more bright was the moonlight,
  For the fields were swathed in snow,
And the moon peered down through pine-trees
  On the hard, white ground below.
But often to aid the moonbeams
  A 'starlight' soared, and fell,
And now and again, to southward,
  The flash of a bursting shell.
Deep, deep black the shadows
  On the hard white surface showed,
Of the tall, steep, wooded hillside
  Above where the Ancre flowed
Out from the German trenches
  Silently through our own,
And we stood by the bank above it,
  Leslie and I, alone.
Near us, a watchful sentry,
  Gazing across the wire,
And three, in a tiny dug-out,
  Crouched round a brazier fire.

We talked, as we stood together,
  As we often before had done,
Of the times we should have together
  When at last the war was won!
Much we planned that evening
  Of the wonderful days in store,
When trench life should be as a nightmare,
  And an ugly dream the war.

You went, old man, before me;
  You died as I knew you, game;
And 'the wonderful days in store' now
  Could never appear the same.
With the best of pals to share them
  What mad, glad days they would be!
But the best of my pals lies buried
  In shell-scarred Picardy.

A cloud drifts over the moon-face,
  And the air has grown more chill;
I turn from the open window
  While the shadow climbs the hill.
But my mind still runs on that evening
  When the moon shone through the pines
That grow by the Ancre River,
  Behind the British lines;
When Leslie and I together
  Stood in the crisp, white snow,
With the dug-out light above us,
  And the running stream below;
And spoke of home and dear ones,
  And mentioned not the war,
But only the days to follow,
  The wonderful days in store.

ERIC FITZWATER WILKINSON

YOUTH IN ARMS

Strange to see, among those thousands of faces I scanned, suddenly a red-haired youth with green eyes looking far away, sidelong – one clean face, among all the others brutalized. But their hearts are gold, I doubt not.

SIEGFRIED SASSOON[127]

TO A BOY

Oh arrow-straight and slender
  With grey eyes unafraid,
You see the roses' splendour
  Nor reck that they shall fade.

Youth in its flush and flower
  Has a soul of whitest flame,
Eternity in an hour,
  All life and death in a game.

May youth for ever weave you
  His magic round your ways,
And Time the robber leave you
  The boy's heart all your days.

W. N. HODGSON

MECHANIC REPAIRING A MOTOR-CYCLE

Something in the look of him makes my pulses snatch.
He crouches on the garage floor beside
The patient engine while I stand and watch.
Black dirt and oil and loose blue clothing hide
What can be hidden. But suddenly streaming wide
The sun's rays enter through the door and catch
His neck and by their alchemy are descried
Grace and glory of youth nowhere to match.

Here is the perfect beauty, not aware
Of its own worth, not asking homage due.
Not like those lads whom sculptor Myron knew,
Whose bodies proudly moved in Grecian air
Bending to conscious play and gleaming bare.
Here's soil and sweat, and youth shines godlike through.

GEOFFREY FABER

ARMS AND THE BOY

Let the boy try along this bayonet-blade
How cold steel is, and keen with hunger of blood;
Blue with all malice, like a madman's flash;
And thinly drawn with famishing for flesh.

Lend him to stroke these blind, blunt bullet-leads
Which long to nuzzle in the hearts of lads,
Or give him cartridges of fine zinc teeth,
Sharp with the sharpness of grief and death.

For his teeth seem for laughing round an apple.
There lurk no claws behind his fingers supple;
And God will grow no talons at his heels,
Nor antlers through the thickness of his curls.

WILFRED OWEN

YOUTH IN ARMS (i)

Happy boy, happy boy,
David the immortal willed,
Youth a thousand thousand times
Slain, but not once killed,
Swaggering again to-day
In the old contemptuous way;

Leaning backward from your thigh
Up against the tinselled bar—
Dust and ashes! is it you?
Laughing, boasting, there you are!
First we hardly recognized you
In your modern avatar.

Soldier, rifle, brown khaki—
Is your blood as happy so?
Where's your sling, or painted shield,
Helmet, pike, or bow?
Well, you're going to the wars—
That is all you need to know.
Greybeards plotted. They were sad.
Death was in their wrinkled eyes.
At their tables, with their maps
Plans and calculations, wise
They all seemed; for well they knew
How ungrudgingly Youth dies.

At their green official baize
They debated all the night
Plans for your adventurous days
Which you followed with delight,
Youth in all your wanderings,
David of a thousand slings.

HAROLD MONRO

THE DUG-OUT

Why do you lie with your legs ungainly huddled,
And one arm bent across your sullen, cold,
Exhausted face? It hurts my heart to watch you,
Deep-shadow'd from the candle's guttering gold;

And you wonder why I shake you by the shoulder;
Drowsy, you mumble and sigh and turn your head . . .
You are too young to fall asleep for ever;
And when you sleep you remind me of the dead.

SIEGFRIED SASSOON

'HARK, HARK, THE LARK'

Hark, hark, the lark to heaven's gate uprisen,
Pours out his joy . . .
I think of you, shut in some distant prison,
O Boy, poor Boy;

Your heart grown sick with hope deferred and shadows
Of prison ways;
Not daring to snatch a thought of Severn meadows,
Or old blue-days.

IVOR GURNEY

SOLDIERS BATHING

White bodies flash by Yser
And happy words are said.
And one-and-twenty's laughter
Rings hollow in my head
Who know that they are dead.

You lad with eyes of April
And promising of May,
You bathe yourself in Yser
Against your burial day
That is not far away.

You strong and hairy sergeant
  Stretched naked to the skies,
The willow herb he crushes
  Shall flame above his eyes;
  His hour is, and he dies.

Their splendid youth is perished.
  They are but ghosts of men—
Light lips and hearts of laughter,
  Eyes that smile not again
  See not threescore and ten.

R. D. GREENWAY

RED WINE

Now seven supple lads and clean
  Sat down to drink one night,
Sat down to drink at Nouex-les-Mines
  And then went off to fight;
And seven supple lads and clean
  Are finished with the fight,
But only three at Nouex-les-Mines
  Sit down to drink to-night.

And when we took the cobbled road
  We often took before,
Our thoughts were with the hearty lads
  Who trod that way no more.
Oh! lads out on the level fields,
  If you could call to mind
The good red wine at Nouex-les-Mines
  You would not stay behind!

And when we left the trench to-night,
Each weary with his load,
Grey, silent ghosts, as light as air,
Came with us down the road.
And now we sit us down to drink
You sit beside us, too,
And drink red wine at Nouex-les-Mines
As once you used to do.

PATRICK MACGILL

TO LIEUT. O'D

(Killed in action at Loos, 1916)

See him standing at the corner,
Cynosure of friendly eyes,
Challenging their kindly sallies,
Combatting with swift replies.

Eyes alight with Life and Laughter,
Brown eyes full of mirth and fun;
Fresh face tanned by months of warfare,
Lithe limbs browned by summer sun.

Suddenly a shell comes screaming,
Through the blue vault overhead,
Strikes – His laughing lips are silent,
All his splendid youth lies dead.

Death! whose arrow countless thousands
And unerring aim have proved,
Could you not have aimed untruly,
Spared for me the boy I loved?

F. S. WOODLEY

STAND DOWN!

I touch his hands. They are cold
And his dear boy lips are grey;
And his eyes have the look of a man grown old
In a tired kind of way.

A deep and lasting sleep.
The 'stand down' of his small share.
The dawn when the still winds creep.—
Dear God! how they lift his hair.

A. NEWBERRY CHOYCE

THE QUESTION

Soldier-boy, at the edge of the wood,
  Stretched on the tufty grass,
With a red wound there in your tangled hair
  And never a friend to pass,

The sky is dark, it will rain to-night,
  And you are not very old,
So I bring green branches to cover you
  And shelter you from the cold.

Soldier-boy, it's a grim old world
  (Deny it, he who can),
Who knows that your life would have happier been,
  Had you lived to be a man?

RICHARD DENNYS

YOUTH IN ARMS (iv)

Carrion

It is plain now what you are. Your head has dropped
Into a furrow. And the lovely curve
Of your strong leg has wasted and is propped
Against a ridge of the ploughed land's watery swerve.

You are swayed on waves of the silent ground;
You clutch and claim with passionate grasp of your fingers
The dip of earth in which your body lingers;
If you are not found,
In a little while your limbs will fall apart;
The birds will take some, but the earth will take most your heart.

You are fuel for a coming spring if they leave you here;
The crop that will rise from your bones is healthy bread.
You died—we know you—without a word of fear,
And as they loved you living I love you dead.

No girl would kiss you. But then
No girls would ever kiss the earth
In the manner they hug the lips of men:
You are not known to them in this, your second birth.

No coffin-cover now will cram
Your body in a shell of lead;
Earth will not fall on you from the spade with a slam,
But will fold and enclose you slowly, you living dead.

Hush, I hear the guns. Are you still asleep?
Surely I saw you a little heave to reply.
I can hardly think you will not turn over and creep
Along the furrows trenchward as if to die.

HAROLD MONRO

THE SOLDIER

My years I counted twenty-one
Mostly at tail of plough:
The furrow that I drove is done,
To sleep in furrow now.

I leapt from living to the dead
A bullet was my bane.
It split the nutshell of my head,
The kernel of my brain.

A lad to life has paid his debts
Who bests and kills a foe,
And man upon his sweetheart gets
To reap as well as sow.

But I shall take no son by hand,
No greybeard bravo be:
My ghost is tethered in the sand
Afar from my degree.

FRANK PREWETT

IN MEMORIAM

Private D. Sutherland killed in action
in the German trench, May 16, 1916,
and the others who died

So you were David's father,
And he was your only son,
And the new-cut peats are rotting
And the work is left undone,
Because of an old man weeping.
Just an old man in pain,
For David, his son David,
That will not come again.

Oh, the letters he wrote you,
And I can see them still,
Not a word of the fighting
But just the sheep on the hill
And how you should get the crops in
Ere the year got stormier,
And the Bosches have got his body,
And I was his officer.

You were only David's father,
But I had fifty sons
When we went up in the evening
Under the arch of the guns,
And we came back at twilight—
O God! I heard them call
To me for help and pity
That could not help at all.

Oh, never will I forget you,
My men that trusted me,
More my sons than your fathers',
For they could only see
The little helpless babies
And the young men in their pride.
They could not see you dying,
And hold you while you died.

Happy and young and gallant,
They saw their first-born go,
But not the strong limbs broken
And the beautiful men brought low,
The piteous writhing bodies,
They screamed, 'Don't leave me, Sir,'
For they were only your fathers
But I was your officer.

E. A. MACKINTOSH

. . . KILLED IN ACTION, 1916

Slight and loose-limbed, blue-eyed, blue-eyed,
Swift and straight as a flower in spring,
Which of his gifts had love denied,
What of his almsgiving?

Over the word and past the sun
Cries the voice of a lover in pain.
Empty the earth, the day is done,
Dawn will not come again.

R. D. GREENWAY

THE GREATER LOVE

A sensible sort of man came in the hut after dinner. Owen of the one-leg, a Ceylon planter who got hit before he'd seen the Dardanelles two days. He asked me why there are no women in my verse. I told him they are outside my philosophy.

SIEGFRIED SASSOON[128]

MY COMPANY (iv–i)

Kenneth Farrar is typical of many:
He smokes his pipe with a glad heart
And makes his days serene;
He fights hard,
And in his speech he hates the Boche:—
But really he doesn't care a damn.
His sexual experience is wide and various
And his curses are rather original.

But I've seen him kiss a dying man;
And if he comes thro' all right
(So he says)
He'll settle down and marry.

HERBERT READ

STILL FROM THE FIRST I KNEW IT WAS A DREAM

Still from the first I knew it was a Dream
Too eager for fulfilment; yet your voice
Could even make it seem
An answer'd Hope, resting on but a Choice.

I was bereav'd, in darkness, and alone,
When you came to me breathing gratitude
For things I had not done,
Your very sight with Friendliness imbued.

And Friendliness was what I wanted most,
Having lost Love.

JAMES S. YATES

FRIENDSHIP

When I would summon words to sing for you,
The tenderness that draws us each to each
Seems over-wise and delicate for speech,
And what are words, a feeble folk and few!
Your hand in mine; enough that this be true;
Your heart to mine, and why should I beseech
The tongues of men and angels? They could teach
Little to Love, and nothing strange or new.

The silence; let the sound of all men's feet,
And all the fret of voices touch us not.
Then Peace, in which these others have no lot,
And Time folds up his wings that were so fleet:
Your hand in mine; only the pulse should beat,
Your heart to mine, and all the world forgot.

J. GRIFFYTH FAIRFAX

THE DEAD SOLDIER

Thy dear brown eyes which were as depths where truth
Lay bowered with frolic joy, but yesterday
Shone with the fire of thy so guileless youth,
Now ruthless death has dimmed and closed for aye.

Those sweet red lips, that never knew the stain
Of angry words or harsh, or thoughts unclean,
Have sung their last gay song. Never again
Shall I the harvest of their laughter glean.

The goodly harvest of thy laughing mouth
Is garnered in; and lo! the golden grain
Of all thy generous thoughts, which knew no drouth
Of meanness, and thy tender words remain

Stored in my heart; and though I may not see
Thy peerless form nor hear thy voice again,
The memory lives of what thou wast to me.
We knew great love . . . We have not lived in vain.

SYDNEY OSWALD

VOICES OF WOMEN

Met ye my love?
Ye might in France have met him;
He has a wooing smile,
Who sees cannot forget him!
Met ye my love?—
—We shared full many a mile.

Saw ye my love?
In lands far-off he has been,
With his yellow-tinted hair,—
In Egypt such ye have seen,
Ye knew my love?—
—I was his brother there.

Heard ye my love?
My love ye must have heard,
For his voice when he will
Tinkles like cry of a bird;
Heard ye my love?—
—We sang on a Grecian hill.

Behold your love,
And how shall I forget him,
His smile, his hair, his song;
Alas, no maid shall get him
For all her love,
Where he sleeps a million strong.

FRANK PREWETT

GREATER LOVE

Red lips are not so red
   As the stained stones kissed by the English dead.
Kindness of wooed and wooer
Seems shame to their love pure.
O Love, your eyes lose lure
   When I behold eyes blinded in my stead!

Your slender attitude
   Trembles not exquisite like limbs knife-skewed,
Rolling and rolling there
Where God seems not to care;
Till the fierce love they bear
   Cramps them in death's extreme decrepitude.

Your voice sings not so soft,—
   Though even as wind murmuring through raftered loft,—
Your dear voice is not dear,
Gentle, and evening clear,
As theirs whom none now hear,
   Now earth has stopped their piteous mouths that coughed.

Heart, you were never hot
   Nor large, nor full like hearts made great with shot;
And though your hand be pale,
Paler are all which trail
Your cross through flame and hail:
   Weep, you may weep, for you may touch them not.

WILFRED OWEN

PASSING THE LOVE OF WOMEN

Yes, I've sat in the summer twilight,
  Wiv a nice girl, 'and in 'and,
But I've thought even then of the shell 'oles,
  Where the boys of the old Bat. stand.
I've turned to 'er lips for 'er kisses,
  And I've found them kisses cold,
Stone cold and pale like a twice-told tale,
  What has gorn all stale and old.
And the light in 'er eyes 'as gorn all faint,
  And the sound of 'er voice grown dim,
As I 'eard the machine guns singin' aht,
  A-singin' their evenin' 'ymn.
Yes, I've known the love ov a woman, lad,
  And maybe I shall again,
But I knows a stronger love than theirs,
  And that is the love of men.
I could keep my cushy billet, lad,
  If I liked to swing the lead,
I could kiss my gal in the gloamin'
  And sleep in a decent bed.
But I've 'eard my comrades callin' aht,
  From across that bit ov sea,
Come back—come back—would ye loaf and slack,
  And leave it to such as we?
Come back—come back—with their old tack-tack,
  I can 'ear the machine guns sing,
Come back—come back—don't skunk and slack,
  For this ain't no time to swing,
Come back—come back into no man's land,
  For that is the land of men,
And no man's land is the true man's land,
  Come back—come back again.
Aye, the love of women draws ye, lad,
  It's the oldest, sweetest spell,
But your comrade Love is stronger love,

'Cause it draws ye back to 'ell.
The love of a woman draws to 'eaven,
An' 'eaven of 'uman bliss,
To the eyes that sing, the arms that cling,
And the long, long lovers' kiss.
But your comrades keeps on callin' ye,
Callin' ye back to 'ell,
To the fear o' death and the chokin' breath,
Drawn thick with a sickly smell.
Gawd knows, old sport, I 'ave loved my lass
As a man should love his mate,
Body and soul I 'ave loved my lass,
But this love's strong—like Fate.
It 'as cut down deep, to see 'er weep,
And she knows I love 'er well,
But I must go back to the old tack-tack,
To my pals and to Bloody 'Ell.

G. A. STUDDERT KENNEDY

THE SECRET

Suddenly with a shy, sad grace
She turns to me her lighted face,
And I who hear some idle phrase
Watch how her wry lips move,
And guess that the poor words they frame
Mean nought, for they would speak the same
Message I read in the dark flame
Within her eyes, which say, 'I love.'
But I can only turn away . . .

I, that have heard the deep voice break
Into a sing-song sobbing shake,
Whose flutter made my being quake,
  What ears have I for women's cries?
I, that have seen the turquoise glaze
Fixed in the blue and quivering gaze
Of one whom cocaine cannot daze,
  How can I yield to woman's eyes?
    I, who can only turn away.

I, that have held strong hands which palter,
Borne the full weight of limbs that falter,
Bound live flesh on the surgeon's altar,
  What need have I of woman's hand?
I, that have felt the dead's embrace;
I, whose arms were his resting-place;
I, that have kissed a dead man's face;
  Ah, but how should you understand?
    Now I can only turn away.

ROBERT NICHOLS

RESERVE

Though you desire me I will still feign sleep
And check my eyes from opening to the day,
For as I lie, thrilled by your dark gold flesh,
I think of how the dead, my dead, once lay.

RICHARD ALDINGTON

FULFILMENT

Was there love once? I have forgotten her.
Was there grief once? grief yet is mine.
Other loves I have, men rough, but men who stir
More grief, more joy, than love of thee and thine.

Faces cheerful, full of whimsical mirth,
Lined by the wind, burned by the sun;
Bodies enraptured by the abounding earth,
As whose children we are brethren: one.

And any moment may descend hot death
To shatter limbs! pulp, tear, blast
Beloved soldiers who love rough life and breath
Not less for dying faithful to the last.

O the fading eyes, the grimed face turned bony,
Oped mouth gushing, fallen head,
Lessening pressure of a hand shrunk, clammed, and stony!
O sudden spasm, release of the dead!

Was there love once? I have forgotten her.
Was there grief once? grief yet is mine.
O loved, living, dying, heroic soldier,
All, all, my joy, my grief, my love, are thine!

ROBERT NICHOLS

From 'TEN YEARS AFTER'

And yet I cannot close
Without some word of those
Who, through long nights and days,
Once stood by me.
O men of mine,
No word repays
That loyalty,
That faith divine
Which ever held you fast
To seek the isles
Where Beauty dwells,
And finding see at last
Its sun-kissed tiles
And citadels.

Through those long years of strife,
When all was dear, but life,
And mists irresolute spread
The way with doubt,
And faintly loomed
The distant height,
While in the rout
Of panic gloomed
Contagion's fearsome hue,
I found in Hell
That love of man
For men—a love more true
Than women tell
Since love began.

Nor can I e'er forget
The valiant deaths you met,
Your patient courage high,
Your thoughts which dwelt
In dying breath
On the day's fate. And I
Who only felt
The wings of Death
Still worship at your shrine:
For all you had
You gave to me—
Your love, your lives were mine,
And yours the glad
Proud chivalry.

On to the bitter end
You went: nothing could bend
Your wayward courage high.
And so you'd meet
At end of day
Death's grim and sudden cry:
Mocking you'd greet
That hopeless fray
With courage still uncowed—
The issue known,
Yet, one more fight—
And then, head still unbowed,
Though overthrown,
Into the Light.

W. G. THOMAS

APOLOGIA PRO POEMATE MEO

I, too, saw God through mud,—
The mud that cracked on cheeks when wretches smiled.
War brought more glory to their eyes than blood,
And gave their laughs more glee than shakes a child.

Merry it was to laugh there—
Where death becomes absurd and life absurder.
For power was on us as we slashed bones bare
Not to feel sickness or remorse of murder.

I, too, have dropped off fear—
Behind the barrage, dead as my platoon,
And sailed my spirit surging light and clear
Past the entanglement where hopes lay strewn;

And witnessed exultation—
Faces that used to curse me, scowl for scowl,
Shine and lift up with passion of oblation,
Seraphic for an hour; though they were foul.

I have made fellowships—
Untold of happy lovers in old song.
For love is not the binding of fair lips
With the soft silk of eyes that look and long,

By Joy, whose ribbon slips,—
But wound with war's hard wire whose stakes are strong;
Bound with the bandage of the arm that drips;
Knit in the webbing of the rifle-thong.

I have perceived much beauty
In the hoarse oaths that kept our courage straight;
Heard music in the silentness of duty;
Found peace where shell-storms spouted reddest spate.

Nevertheless, except you share
With them in hell the sorrowful dark of hell,
Whose world is but the trembling of a flare,
And heaven but as the highway for a shell,

You shall not hear their mirth:
You shall not come to think them well content
By any jest of mine. These men are worth
Your tears. You are not worth their merriment.

WILFRED OWEN

EPILOGUE

Che son contenti nel fuoco

We are of those that Dante saw
Glad, for love's sake, among the flames of hell,
Outdaring with a kiss all-powerful wrath;
For we have passed athwart a fiercer hell,
Through gloomier, more desperate circles
Than ever Dante dreamed:
And yet love kept us glad.

RICHARD ALDINGTON

THE TRIUMPH

When life was a cobweb of stars for Beauty who came
In the whisper of leaves or a bird's lone cry in the glen,
On dawn-lit hills and horizons girdled with flame
I sought for the triumph that troubles the faces of men.

With death in the terrible flickering gloom of the fight
I was cruel and fierce with despair; I was naked and bound;
I was stricken: and Beauty returned through the shambles of night;
In the faces of men she returned; and their triumph I found.

SIEGFRIED SASSOON

SHADOW AND LIGHT

Last night the moon was like a golden shield
On a star-powdered arras; to and fro
A hundred swords of leaping light below,
Crossing and flashing, filled the airy field.
To our eyes watching was their way revealed
To search all heaven, in hatred, for a foe:
But we, far under, had more wit to know
How Love in shadow looks for Love concealed.

There is no dark so dark I would not find
Light in your eyes enough to read thereby
Beauty and Truth. A venerable lie
Was handed down by Time that Love is blind,
But the God laughs, and keeps a tranquil mind,
And we know better—Love, and you, and I.

J. GRIFFYTH FAIRFAX

SECRET MUSIC

I keep such music in my brain
No din this side of death can quell;
Glory exulting over pain,
And beauty, garlanded in hell.

My dreaming spirit will not heed
The roar of guns that would destroy
My life that on the gloom can read
Proud-surging melodies of joy.

To the world's end I went, and found
Death in his carnival of glare;
But in my torment I was crowned,
And music dawned above despair.

SIEGFRIED SASSOON

THE ENEMY

He is the only German soldier I can now clearly visualize . . . a tall, pale, plump, blond, young Teuton of my own age or a little more. He lay as he had fallen, in an attitude of running, struck by three shrapnel bullets in the back – not running away but carrying a message, for in his hand was a dirty scrap of paper on which three words were scribbled: '*die Engländer kommen*'. His grey eyes were open, and his mouth showed strong white teeth. I looked on him and loved him.

CHARLES CARRINGTON[129]

GERMAN PRISONERS

When first I saw you in the curious street,
Like some platoon of soldier ghosts in grey,
My mad impulse was all to smite and slay,
To spit upon you—tread you 'neath my feet.
But when I saw how each sad soul did greet
My gaze with no sign of defiant frown,
How from tired eyes looked spirits broken down,
How each face showed the pale flag of defeat,
And doubt, despair, and disillusionment,
And how were grievous wounds on many a head,
And on your garb red-faced was other red;
And how you stooped as men whose strength was spent,
I knew that we had suffered each as other,
And could have grasped your hand and cried, 'My brother'!

JOSEPH LEE

LIEDHOLZ

When I captured Liedholz
I had a blackened face
Like a nigger's,
And my teeth like white mosaics shone.

We met in the night at half-past one,
Between the lines.
Liedholz shot at me
And I at him;
And in the ensuing tumult he surrendered to me.

Before we reached our wire
He told me he had a wife and three children.
In the dug-out we gave him a whiskey.
Going to the Brigade with my prisoner at dawn,
The early sun made the land delightful,
And larks rose singing from the plain.

In broken French we discussed
Beethoven, Nietzsche and the International.

He was a professor
Living at Spandau;
And not too intelligible.

But my black face and nigger's teeth
Amused him.

HERBERT READ

OFTEN WHEN WARRING

Often when warring for he wist not what,
An enemy-soldier, passing by one weak,
Has tendered water, wiped the burning cheek,
And cooled the lips so black and clammed and hot;

Then gone his way, and maybe quite forgot
The deed of grace amid the roar and reek;
Yet larger vision than the tongue can speak
He there has reached, although he has known it not.

For natural mindsight, triumphing in the act
Over the throes of artificial rage,
Has thereby muffled victory's peal of pride,
Rended to ribands policy's specious page
That deals but with evasion, code, and pact,
And war's apology wholly stultified.

THOMAS HARDY

BALLAD OF THE BAYONETS

It was a fearsome way, and long,
Where we met fact to face.
From end to end a demon song
Rolled on above while the bloody throng
Of the dead beneath kept pace.

We met, and each drove in the steel
With yell of maniac hate;
Mine clave his body through, and the feel
Of the riven flesh was a thunder peal
From the sounding domes of fate.

His took me fair: where the heart had lain
There sucked the sickening point,
And all the world was a reeling pain,
And all earth dark with a shameful stain
No honour could anoint.

We fell, and lay there side by side,
In that strange and fearsome place.
The lonely soul gave up its pride
Before the black mouth opening wide
Of cold and shrieking space.

The lonely soul gave up its pride:
With the last thing we knew,
Each reached a fumbling hand and sighed
A 'Brother' out, before he died,
'—Brother! I go with you.'

'HARRY BRANDER'
(Eva Mudocci)

THE EFFECT

The effect of our bombardment was terrific. One man told me he had never seen so many dead before.—*War Correspondent.*

'He'd never seen so many dead before.'
They sprawled in yellow daylight while he swore
And gasped and lugged his everlasting load
Of bombs along what once had been a road.
'How peaceful are the dead.'
Who put that silly gag in someone's head?

'He'd never seen so many dead before.'
The lilting words danced up and down his brain,
While corpses jumped and capered in the rain.
No, no; he wouldn't count them any more . . .
The dead have done with pain:
They've choked; they can't come back to life again.

When Dick was killed last week he looked like that,
Flapping along the fire-step like a fish,
After the blazing crump had knocked him flat . . .
'How many dead? As many as ever you wish.
Don't count 'em; they're too many.
Who'll buy my nice fresh corpses, two a penny?'

SIEGFRIED SASSOON

LAST NOCTURNE

The searchlight swords
Stab the sky
Miles back,
Like taut cords
Of gold, high
Against the black.

A star-flare
Of showering red
Surprises night,
And hangs in air,
Painting the dead
With ruddy light.

The pale wax
Of their faces
Turns to blood
By dim tracks
In dark places
Of the wood

Where I go
Hurrying on.
Suddenly
I stumble low
On some one.
God on high!

His face was cold,
And very white;
There was no blood.
I grew old
That night
In the wood.

He was young,
My enemy—
But lips the same
As lips have sung
Often with me.
I whispered the name

Of the friend whose face
Was so like his;
But never a sound
In the dim place
Under the trees
Closing round.

Then I cursed
My Nocturnes—
I hated night;
Hated it worst
When the moon turns
Her tired light

On horrible things
Man has done
With life and love.
Only a fool sings
When night's begun
And the moon's above.

I cursed each song
I made for men
Full of moonlight
Lasting night-long;
For I knew then
How evil is night.

I cursed each tune
Of night-dim wood
And Naiad's stream,
By that mad moon
Asearch for blood
And the waxen gleam

Of dead faces
Under the trees
In the trampled grass,
Till the bloody traces
Of the agonies
Of night-time pass.

H. L. SIMPSON

GERMAN BOY

German boy with cold blue eyes,
In the cold and blue moonrise.
I who live and still shall know
Flowers that smell and winds that blow,
I who live to walk again,
Fired the shot that broke your brain.

By your hair all stiff with blood,
By your lips befouled with mud,
By your dreams that shall no more
Leave the nest and sing and soar,
By the children never born
From your body smashed and torn,
—When I too shall stand at last
In the deadland vast,
Shall you heap upon my soul
Agonies of coal?
Shall you bind my throat with cords,
Stab me through with swords?
Or shall you be gentler far
Than a bird or than a star?
Shall you know that I was bound
In the noose that choked you round?
Shall you say, 'The way was hid.

Lord, he knew not what he did'?
Shall your eyes that day be mild,
Like the Sacrifice, the Child?
. . . German boy with cold blue eyes,
In the cold and blue moonrise.

LOUIS GOLDING

THE DEAD TURK

Dead, dead, and dumbly chill. He seemed to lie
Carved from the earth, in beauty without stain.
And suddenly
Day turned to night, and I beheld again
A still Centurion with eyes ablaze:
And Calvary re-echoed with his cry—
His cry of stark amaze.

GEOFFREY DEARMER

THE GERMAN GRAVES

I wonder are there roses still
In Ablain St Nazaire,
And crosses girt with daffodil
In that old garden there.
I wonder if the long grass waves
With wild-flowers just the same
Where the Germans made their soldiers' graves
Before the English came?

The English set those crosses straight
  And kept the legends clean;
The English made the wicket-gate
  And left the garden green;
And now who knows what regiments dwell
  In Ablain St Nazaire?
But I would have them guard as well
  The graves we guarded there.

So do not tear those fences up
  And drive your waggons through,
Or trample rose and buttercup
  As careless feet may do;
For I have friends where Germans tread
  In graves across the line,
And as I do towards their dead
  So may they do to mine.

And when at last the Prussians pass
  Among those mounds and see
The reverent cornflowers crowd the grass
  Because of you and me,
They'll give perhaps one humble thought
  To all the 'English fools'
Who fought as never men have fought
  But somehow kept the rules.

A. P. HERBERT

ENEMIES

He stood alone in some queer sunless place
Where Armageddon ends; perhaps he longed
For days he might have lived; but his young face
Gazed forth untroubled: and suddenly there thronged
Round him the hulking Germans that I shot
When for his death my brooding rage was hot.

He stared at them, half-wondering; and then
They told him how I'd killed them for his sake,—
Those patient, stupid, sullen ghosts of men:
And still there seemed no answer he could make.
At last he turned and smiled, and all was well
Because his face could lead them out of hell.

SIEGFRIED SASSOON

STRANGE MEETING

It seemed that out of battle I escaped
Down some profound dull tunnel, long since scooped
Through granites which titanic wars had groined.
Yet also there encumbered sleepers groaned,
Too fast in thought or death to be bestirred.
Then, as I probed them, one sprang up, and stared
With piteous recognition in fixed eyes,
Lifting distressful hands as if to bless.
And by his smile, I knew that sullen hall,
By his dead smile I knew we stood in Hell.
With a thousand pains that vision's face was grained;
Yet no blood reached there from the upper ground,
And no guns thumped, or down the flues made moan.
'Strange friend,' I said, 'here is no cause to mourn.'
'None,' said the other, 'save the undone years,
The hopelessness. Whatever hope is yours,
Was my life also; I went hunting wild
After the wildest beauty in the world,
Which lies not calm in eyes, or braided hair,
But mocks the steady running of the hour,
And if it grieves, grieves richlier than here.
For of my glee might many men have laughed,
And of my weeping something had been left,
Which must die now. I mean the truth untold,
The pity of war, the pity war distilled.

Now men will go content with what we spoiled,
Or, discontent, boil bloody, and be spilled.
They will be swift with swiftness of the tigress.
None will break ranks, though nations trek from progress.
Courage was mine, and I had mystery,
Wisdom was mine, and I had mastery:
To miss the march of this retreating world
Into vain citadels that are not walled.
Then, when much blood had clogged their chariot-wheels,
I would go up and wash them from sweet wells,
Even with truths that lie too deep for taint.
I would have poured my spirit without stint

But not through wounds; not on the cess of war.
Foreheads of men have bled where no wounds were.
I am the enemy you killed, my friend.
I knew you in this dark: for so you frowned
Yesterday through me as you jabbed and killed.
I parried; but my hands were loath and cold.
Let us sleep now . . .'

WILFRED OWEN

THE DEAD

In the half-clouded moonlight the parson stood above the graves, and everything was dim but the striped flag laid across them. Robert Graves, beside me, with his white whimsical face twisted and grieving. Once we could not hear the solemn words for the noise of a machine-gun along the line; and when all was finished a canister fell a few hundred yards away to burst with a crash. So Tommy left us, a gentle soldier, perfect and without stain. And so he will always remain in my heart, fresh and happy and brave.

SIEGFRIED SASSOON[130]

BY THE RIVER

We walked together on a certain day,
If you remember—
And out of a cloudless sky
Death the Jester
Touched us, and smiled and passed.

But a second time you walked with Death.
This time you walked alone—
And he would not let you go.

Sometimes I see your face in the river,
For the river flows always past me where I sit,
And therein move many faces.
Yours I know because of the eyes
With the far look where no fear is,
Neither doubt, nor any sorrow.

Surely you have found peace there,
In the river,
As I also peace beside it,
Watching the moving faces,
With no fear, no doubt, no sorrow,
Sure of the Sea.

J. GRIFFYTH FAIRFAX

MISSING: UNOFFICIALLY REPORTED KILLED

Was it in the noonday that you left us,
  When the ranks were wrapped in smoke?
Or did you pass unnoticed on the midnight,
  Ere the chiller morning broke?

Did the lust and heat of battle find you ready,
  Shoulders braced and heart aflame?
Or did death steal by and take you unexpected,
  When the final summons came?

Not amidst the companies and clamour
  Of this horror men call War,
Where man, the godlike, tramples down his fellows
  To the dust they were before;

But on some still November morning
  When the frost was in the air,
Noiselessly your strong soul took its passing,
  And I, your friend, not there—not there!

Silently the dead leaves swing and settle
  In their appointed place;
The season of the singing birds is over,
  The winter sets apace.

Somewhere in the ruin of the autumn,
  When the hosts of war are sped,
They will find you, 'midst the quiet wondering faces
  Of the unnumbered dead.

J. L. CROMMELIN BROWN

A MAN'S MAN

(To * * * * killed in action)

I called his name—he did not heed my calling,
I tried to feel his hand grip mine again;
O God, I could not keep the tears from falling
Although I smiled to hide the bitter pain.

All that is past, but still I hear his laughter—
Glad echoes from the days before he went,
I did not know such pain could follow after
His splendid life so true and nobly spent.

He was a man . . . I linger where his cross
Shines white among the shadows, and I know
My very soul is strengthened by my loss.
My comrade still in death—I loved him so.

RAYMOND HEYWOOD

DICKY

(to his memory)

They found him when the day
Was yet but gloom;
Six feet of scarréd clay
Was ample room
And wide enough domain for all desires
For him, whose glowing eyes
Made mock at lethargies,
Were not a moment still;—
Can Death, all slayer, kill
The fervent source of those exultant fires?
Nay, not so;
Somewhere that glow
And starry shine so clear astonishes yet
The wondering spirits as they come and go.
Eyes that nor they nor we shall ever forget.

IVOR GURNEY

THE DEAD LOVER

Were you quick and active once—you that lie so still?
Did your brain run nimbly once, your lungs expand and fill?
Were problems worth the trying, was living worth the dying?
Did the flying moment pay you for the labour up the hill?

Ah, you stay so silent now! you could tell me why
Woods are green in April now, and men are made to die.
Do you feel the spring, I wonder, through the turf you're sleeping
  under,
Though the thunder and the sunshine cannot reach you where you
  lie?

The good rain trickles down to you and laps your limbs about,
The young grass has its roots in you, your bones and members sprout.
Ah, poor untimely lover, in new fashion you'll discover
That clover still is fragrant, and the primroses are out.

Though the old uneasy feeling cannot wake you sleeping there,
Nor the soft spring breezes dally with your crisp delightful hair,
Yet the flowers are round you clinging, and the dust about you
  springing,
And your singing spirit wanders like an essence on the air.

J. L. CROMMELIN BROWN

NOT DEAD

Walking through trees to cool my heat and pain,
I know that David's with me here again.
All that is simple, happy, strong, he is.
Caressingly I stroke
Rough bark of the friendly oak.
A brook goes bubbling by: the voice is his.

Turf burns with pleasant smoke;
I laugh at chaffinch and at primroses.
All that is simple, happy, strong, he is.
Over the whole wood in a little while
Breaks his slow smile.

ROBERT GRAVES

from 'THE LAST MEETING'

III

I know that he is lost among the stars,
And may return no more but in their light.
Though his hushed voice may call me in the stir
Of whispering trees, I shall not understand.
Men may not speak with stillness; and the joy
Of brooks that leap and tumble down green hills
Is faster than their feet; and all their thoughts
Can win no meaning from the talk of birds.

My heart is fooled with fancies, being wise;
For fancy is the gleaming of wet flowers
When the hid sun looks forth with golden stare.
Thus, when I find new loveliness to praise,
And things long-known shine out in sudden grace,
Then will I think: 'He moves before me now.'
So he will never come but in delight,
And, as it was in life, his name shall be
Wonder awaking in a summer dawn,
And youth, that dying, touched my lips to song.

SIEGFRIED SASSOON

TO LESLIE

(Captain L. C. Hossell: killed in action, August 1916)

Sleep deep, sleep well;
Your requiem knell
The whine and drone of passing shell.
Come cold, come rain,
Their grip is vain,
For you have passed beyond all pain.
Sleep deep, sleep well.

Sleep sound, sleep deep;
Our watch we keep,
And little chance have we to sleep.
Your watch is done;
Your rest begun;
The long, long rest you nobly won.
Sleep sound, sleep deep.

ERIC FITZWATER WILKINSON

TO A FALLEN COMRADE

I heard the voice of Spring come softly pleading
  Across the fresh and breathing wold to-day:
The sun, set free from cloudy bonds, was speeding
  To greet the earth with each impassioned ray.

Wide-flung my casement in the cool I listened!
  The birds were busy toying with a song,
And far afield where dappled grasses glistened
  The meadow brook was murmuring along.

And then there came a bee with yet the numbing
Languors of the winter on its wings:
It turned to gold the quiet with its humming—
And then resumed its drowsy wanderings.

I looked upon the fields and trees and hedges
And saw before mine eyes a world reborn,
And on beyond the green world's utmost edges . . .
Where Hope retreated bleeding and forlorn!

Ah! then I knew that Spring would only bring me
Blue skies and songs and flowers drenched with dew!
Ah! then I knew that Spring could never bring me
The friend I had and, having, lost in you!

MURRAY MCCLYMONT

LOST IN FRANCE

Jo's Requiem

He had the ploughman's strength
in the grasp of his hand:
He could see a crow
three miles away,
and the trout beneath the stone.
He could hear the green oats growing,
and the south-west wind make rain.
He could hear the wheel upon the hill
when it left the level road.
He could make a gate, and dig a pit,
And plough as straight as stone can fall.
And he is dead.

ERNEST RHYS

ELEGY

(For J.N., died of wounds, October 1916)

So you are dead. We lived three months together,
But in these years how absence can divide!
We did not meet again. I wonder whether
You thought of me at all before you died.

There in that whirl of unaccustomed faces,
Strange, friendless, ill, I found in you a friend
And then at last in these divided places
You there in France, I here—and this the end.

For friendship's memory was short and faithless
And time went by that would not come again,
And you are dead of wounds and I am scatheless
Save as my heart has sorrowed for my slain.

I wonder whether you were long in dying,
Where, in what trench, and under what dim star,
With drawn face on the clayey bottom lying,
While still the untiring guns cried out afar.

I might have been with you, I might have seen you
Reel to the shot with blank and staring eye,
I might have held you up . . . I might have been you
And lain instead of you where now you lie.

Here in our quietude strange fancy presses,
Dark thoughts of woe upon the empty brain,
And fills the streets and the pleasant wildernesses
With forms of death and ugly shapes of pain.

You are long dead. A year is nearly over,
But still your voice leaps out again amid
The tangled memories that lie and cover
With countless trails what then we said and did.

And still in waking dreams I sit and ponder
  Pleasures that were and, as my working brain
Deeper in revery will stray and wander,
  I think that I shall meet with you again

And make my plans and half arrange the meeting,
  And half think out the words that will be said
After the first brief, careless pleasant greeting . . .
  Then suddenly I remember you are dead.

EDWARD SHANKS

TO HIS LOVE

He's gone, and all our plans
  Are useless indeed.
We'll walk no more on Cotswold
  Where the sheep feed
  Quietly and take no heed.

His body that was so quick
  Is not as you
Knew it, on Severn river
  Under the blue
  Driving our small boat through.

You would not know him now . . .
  But still he died
Nobly, so cover him over
  With violets of pride
  Purple from Severn side.

Cover him, cover him soon!
  And with thick-set
Masses of memoried flowers—
  Hide that red wet
  Thing I must somehow forget.

IVOR GURNEY

LAMENT IN 1915 (B.H.W.)

I call you, and I call you. Oh come home,
You lonely creature. Curse the foreign clown
Who plugged you with that lead, and knocked you down.
Stand up again and laugh, you wandering friend;
Say, as you would: 'It's just a little hole;
It will soon mend.'
Walk now into the room. Come! Come! Come! Come!

Come! we will laugh together all the night.
(We shall have poured ourselves a glass or two.)
Sit down. Our mutual mirth will reach its height
When we remember how they called you dead,
And I shall ask you how it felt, and you—
'Oh nothing. Just a tumble. Rather hot,
The feeling in my side; and then my head
A trifle dizzy, but I'm back again.
I lay out there too long, and I've still got,
When I think of it, just a little pain.'

I know the way you tumbled . . . Once you slid
And landed on your side. I noticed then
A trick of falling; some peculiar glide—
A curious movement, not like other men.
But did your mouth drop open? Did your breath
Hurt you? What sort of feeling quickly came,
When you discovered that it might be death?

And what will happen if I shout your name?
Perhaps you may be there behind the door,
And if I raise my voice a little more,
You'll swing it open. I don't know how thick
The black partition is between us two.
Answer, if you can hear me; friend, be quick . . .
Listen, the door-bell rang! Perhaps it's you.

You're in the room. You're sitting in that chair.
You are! . . . I will go down. It *was* the bell.
You *may* be waiting at the door as well.

Am I not certain I shall find you there? . . .

You're rigged in your best uniform to-day;
You take a momentary martial stand,
Then step inside and hold me out your hand,
And laugh in that old solitary way.

You don't know why you did it. Al this while
You've slaved and sweated. Now you're very strong,
And so you tell me with a knowing smile:
'We're going out to Flanders before long.'
I thought you would come back with an ugly hole
Below your thigh,
And ask for sympathy and wander lame;
I thought you'ld be that same
Grumbling companion without self-control—
I never thought you'ld die.

* * *

Now let us both forget this brief affair:
Let us begin our friendship all again.
I'm going down to meet you on the stair.
Walk to me! Come! for I can see you plain.
How strange! A moment I did think you dead.
How foolish of me!
Friend! Friend! Are you dumb?
Why are you pale? Why do you hang your head?
You see me? Here's my hand. Why don't you come?
Don't make me angry. You are there, I know.
Is not my house your house? There is a bed
Upstairs. You're tired. Lie down; you must come home.
Some men are killed . . . not you. Be as you were.

And yet—Somehow it's dark down all the stair.
I'm standing at the door. You are not there.

HAROLD MONRO

TO S.A.

I loved you, so I drew these tides of men into my hands
and wrote my will across the sky in stars
To earn you Freedom, the seven pillared worthy house,
that your eyes might be shining for me
When we came.

Death seemed my servant on the road, till we were near
and saw you waiting:
When you smiled, and in sorrowful envy he outran me
and took you apart:
Into his quietness.

Love, the way-weary, groped to your body, our brief wage
ours for the moment
Before earth's soft hand explored your shape, and the blind
worms grew fat upon
Your substance.

Men prayed me that I set our work, the inviolate house,
as a memory of you.
But for fit monument I shattered it, unfinished: and now
The little things creep out to patch themselves hovels
in the marred shadow
Of your gift.

T. E. LAWRENCE

THE DEAD MEN

It was yesterday I heard again
The dead man talk with living men,
And watched the thread of converse go
Among the speakers to and fro,
Woven with merriment and wit
And beauty to embroider it;
And in the middle now and then,
The laughter clear of happy men—
Only to me a charnel scent
Drifted across the argument,
Only to me his fair young head
Was lifeless and untenanted,
And in his quiet even tones,
I heard the sound of naked bones,
And in his empty eyes could see
The man who talked was dead, like me.

Then in the conversation's swim,
I leaned across and spoke to him,
And in his dim and dreary eyes
Read suddenly a strange surprise,
And in the touch of his dank hand,
Knew that he too could understand;
So we two talked, and as we heard
Our friends' applause of each dull word
We felt the slow and mournful winds
Blow through the corpse house of our minds,
And the cool dark of underground.
And all the while they sat around
Weighing each listless thing we said,
And did not know that we were dead.

E. A. MACKINTOSH

I STOOD WITH THE DEAD

I stood with the Dead, so forsaken and still:
When dawn was grey I stood with the Dead.
And my slow heart said, 'You must kill, you must kill:
'Soldier, soldier, morning is red.'

On the shapes of the slain in their crumpled disgrace
I stared for a while through the thin cold rain . . .
'O lad that I loved, there is rain on your face,
'And your eyes are blurred and sick like the plain.'

I stood with the Dead. . . . They were dead; they were dead;
My heart and my head beat a march of dismay:
And gusts of the wind came dulled by the guns.
'Fall in!' I shouted; 'Fall in for your pay!'

SIEGFRIED SASSOON

BACK HOME

I hope you are as warm as I am; as serene in your room as I am here; and that you think of me never in bed as resignedly as I think of you always in bed. Of this I am certain, you could not be visited by a band of friends half so fine as surround me here.

WILFRED OWEN[131]

SICK LEAVE

When I'm asleep, dreaming and lulled and warm,—
They come, the homeless ones, the noiseless dead.
While the dim charging breakers of the storm
Bellow and drone and rumble overhead,
Out of the gloom they gather about my bed.
  They whisper to my heart; their thoughts are mine.
  'Why are you here with all your watches ended?
  From Ypres to Frise we sought you in the Line.'
In bitter safety I awake, unfriended;
And while the dawn begins with slashing rain
I think of the Battalion in the mud.
'When are you going out to them again?
Are they not still your brothers through our blood?'

SIEGFRIED SASSOON

FROM HOME

To the men who fell at Beaumont-Hamel

The pale sun woke in the eastern sky
And a veil of mist was drawn
Over the faces of death and fame
When you went up in the dawn.
With never a thought of fame or death,
Only the work to do,
When you went over the top, my friends,
And I not there with you.

The veil is rent with a rifle-flash
And shows me plain to see
Battle and bodies of men that lived
And fought along with me.
Oh God! it would not have been so hard
If I'd been in it too,
But you are lying stiff, my friends,
And I not there with you.

So here I sit in a pleasant room
By a comfortable fire,
With every thing that a man could want,
But not the heart's desire.
So I sit thinking and dreaming still,
A dream that won't come true,
Of you in the German trench, my friends,
And I not there with you.

E. A. MACKINTOSH

TOASTS AND MEMORIES

(To the Men of the 2/5 Gloucester Regiment)

When once I sat in estaminets
  With trusty friends of mine,
We drank to folk in England
  And pledged them well in wine,

While thoughts of Gloucester filled us—
  Roads against windy skies
At sunset, Severn river,
  Red inn-blinds, country cries.

That stung the heart with sorrow
   And barbéd sweet delight
At Riez Bailleul, Laventie,
   At Merville, many a night.

Now I am over Channel
   I cannot help but think
Of friends who stifle longing
   With friendly food and drink.

'Where's Gurney now, I wonder,
   That smoked a pipe all day;
Sometimes that talked like blazes,
   Sometimes had naught to say?'

And I, at home, must wonder
   Where all my comrades are:
Those men whose Heart-of-Beauty
   Was never stained by War.

IVOR GURNEY

BANISHMENT

I am banished from the patient men who fight.
They smote my heart to pity, built my pride.
Shoulder to aching shoulder, side by side,
They trudged away from life's broad wealds of light.
Their wrongs were mine; and ever in my sight
They went arrayed in honour. But they died,—
Not one by one: and mutinous I cried
To those who sent them out into the night.

The darkness tells how vainly I have striven
To free them from the pit where they must dwell
In outcast gloom convulsed and jagged and riven
By grappling guns. Love drove me to rebel.
Love drives me back to grope with them through hell;
And in their tortured eyes I stand forgiven.

SIEGFRIED SASSOON

BY THE WOOD

How still the day is, and the air how bright!
A thrush sings and is silent in the wood;
The hillside sleeps dizzy with heat and light;
A rhythmic murmur fills the quietude;
A woodpecker prolongs his leisured flight,
Rising and falling on the solitude.

But there are those who far from yon wood lie,
Buried within the trench where all were found.
A weight of mould oppresses every eye,
Within that cabin close their limbs are bound,
And there they rot amid the long profound,
Disastrous silence of grey earth and sky.

These once, too, rested where now rests but one,
Who scarce can lift his panged and heavy head,
Who drinks in grief the hot light of the sun,
Whose eyes watch dully the green branches spread,
Who feels his currents ever slowlier run,
Whose lips repeat a silent '. . . Dead! all dead!'

O youths to come shall drink air warm and bright,
Shall hear the bird cry in the sunny wood,
All my Young England fell to-day in fight:
That bird, that wood, was ransomed by our blood!

I pray you when the drum rolls let your mood
Be worthy of our deaths and your delight.

ROBERT NICHOLS

THE KIND GHOSTS

She sleeps on soft, last breaths; but no ghost looms
Out of the stillness of her palace wall,
Her wall of boys on boys and dooms on dooms.

She dreams of golden gardens and sweet glooms,
Not marvelling why her roses never fall
Nor what red mouths were torn to make their blooms.

The shades keep down which well might roam her hall.
Quiet their blood lies in her crimson rooms
And she is not afraid of their footfall.

They move not from her tapestries, their pall,
Nor pace her terraces, their hecatombs,
Lest aught she be disturbed, or grieved at all.

WILFRED OWEN

OVER IN FLANDERS . . .

They were writing for the Poetry bookshops,
Poetry no doubt well worth reading.
Over in Flanders, in the wet weather,
Love lay bleeding!

If you carefully record your emotions,
Lyric or Sonnet that haunts your head,
Will you revive for me over in Flanders
Love stone dead?

LOUIS GOLDING

CASUALTY LIST

I

Will they never stop their chattering,
throwing misty drifts of words
over the bottomless pit
of their ignorance and my pain? . . .

I will go away.

I will be quiet for a little while,
and there will be no words to trouble the silence . . .

The jessamine in the silver vase is still,
each little starry face is still.

Only the firelight glows,
winks and shivers and glows again,
up and down the sides of the silver vase.

Like the red heart of pity . . .

The little jessamine faces
are sad,
thinking of . . .
I remember.

II

A number, a name, a place . . .

Perhaps he was asleep,

or else talking of Léontine
of Watou,
(missing his esses,
in that way he had,
queer and pleasant,
ever since a Turk bullet hit him in the mouth)

Or singing rag-time with the other men,
when they got him.

Just some little trivial thing,
done every day,
and twenty times a day,
splashed suddenly with blood and dirt,
and so made the finale
of thirty ordinary years.

III

There is nothing in the quietness
save a dull ache,
and a fury at the silliness of it all.

After all, his life was grey;
and even a splash of blood at the latter end
couldn't make death less grey.

There is only fury at the thought
of the obvious murderous silliness of his death,
the stupid mess of his life
in a dull circle of grey little pleasures,
and toil . . .

And I know
that HE, the innermost self of him,
was a thing to know and love.
A thing that all the greyness had not crushed
to its absolute likeness.

O! a man to love, a brother.

IV

But in six years or so? . . .

Dullness and dirtiness and toil
had finally made him their own . . .

How long, how long
shall there be Something
that can grind the faces of poor men
to an ultimate uniformity of dullness
and grinning trivial meanness?

Or pitchfork them at will
(cheering and singing patriotic doggerel)
to a stinking hell,

to crash about for a little,
noisily, miserably;
till the inevitable comes,
and crushes them
bloodily, meanly?

V

The jessamine faces are very still,
waiting, waiting.

The fire gleams
up and down the side
of the cold silver vase,

angrily,
like a fierce threat,
like a terrible rose
suddenly born out of the utter greyness of things.

H. L. SIMPSON

CONCERT

These antique prostitutions—
I deplore my own vague cynicism,
Undressing with indifferent eyes each girl,
Seeing them naked on that paltry stage
Stared at by half a thousand lustful eyes.

These antique prostitutions—
Am I dead? Withered? Grown old?
That not the least flush of desire
Tinges my unmoved flesh,
And that instead of women's living bodies
I see dead men—you understand?—dead men
With sullen, dark red gashes
Luminous in a foul trench?

These antique prostitutions.

RICHARD ALDINGTON

SUICIDE IN THE TRENCHES

I knew a simple soldier boy
Who grinned at life in empty joy,
Slept soundly through the lonesome dark,
And whistled early with the lark.

In winter trenches, cowed and glum,
With crumps and lice and lack of rum,
He put a bullet through his brain.
No one spoke of him again.

You smug-faced crowds with kindling eye
Who cheer when soldier lads march by,
Sneak home and pray you'll never know
The hell where youth and laughter go.

SIEGFRIED SASSOON

DIED OF WOUNDS

And so there fell upon him at the last
All he had feared most, pain and weariness
Exceeding what he feared, until the redress
Of death . . .
My thought goes writhing through his past.
Dear delicate friend, how the world mastered you.
My heart cries after your remembered ways
In the dim firelight and the autumn dark,
Such solitude as once between the two
Of us was shared. How still now would I hark
To your sweet-mannered voice and tempered praise.
But that's no more; the letter on my knee
Says it's no more, and all that quiet wealth
Of mortal spirit and body spent in vain.
It reads not like you: 'Wounded in Gallipoli,
Leading his men' . . .
Had you gone out by stealth,
Closing the door; but this—God's ways aren't plain.

GEOFFREY FABER

AS THE TEAM'S HEAD-BRASS

As the team's head-brass flashed out on the turn
The lovers disappeared into the wood.
I sat among the boughs of the fallen elm
That strewed an angle of the fallow, and
Watched the plough narrowing a yellow square
Of charlock. Every time the horses turned
Instead of treading me down, the ploughman leaned
Upon the handles to say or ask a word,
About the weather, next about the war.
Scraping the share he faced towards the wood,
And screwed along the furrow till the brass flashed
Once more.
                    The blizzard felled the elm whose crest
I sat in, by a woodpecker's round hole,
The ploughman said. 'When will they take it away?'
'When the war's over.' So the talk began—
One minute and an interval of ten,
A minute more and the same interval.
'Have you been out?' 'No.' 'And don't want to, perhaps?'
'If I could only come back again, I should.
I could spare an arm. I shouldn't want to lose
A leg. If I should lose my head, why, so,
I should want nothing more . . . Have many gone
From here?' 'Yes.' 'Many lost?' 'Yes: good few.
Only two teams work on the farm this year.
One of my mates is dead. The second day
In France they killed him. It was back in March,
The very night of the blizzard, too. Now if
He had stayed here we should have moved the tree.'
'And I should not have sat here. Everything
Would have been different. For it would have been
Another world.' 'Ay, and a better, though
If we could see all all might seem good.' Then
The lovers came out of the wood again:
The horses started and for the last time

I watched the clods crumple and topple over
After the ploughshare and the stumbling team.

EDWARD THOMAS

NEWS

They came, you know, and told me you were dead,
Those little men who never dreamed of pain.
'There's not much racing news to-day,' I said.
I said, 'I hope it will be fine again.'
And then, I think, I climbed a certain hill
And saw two plough-shares and a rusty bin,
And further on, beyond John Farmer's mill,
A fence in which five rails had fallen in,
But sixty-two I counted upright still.
And all the time my feet were saying 'dead,'
Beating it slowly, beating through my head.

I saw it all. I saw the little room
In which, they said, they laid you; to and fro
I heard the creeper rustling, and the boom
Of some old hornet on the lawns below.
I saw 'The Stag at Evening' by the door,
And, though I struggled hard, my eye was drawn
On past those old red ink stains on the floor,
On past the table, and 'The Wounded Fawn'
To that bright hair . . .
No, I was wrong before.
Look at those railings, there are sixty-three,
I missed the one beyond laburnum tree.

GODFREY ELTON

A PRIVATE

This ploughman dead in battle slept out of doors
Many a frozen night, and merrily
Answered staid drinkers, good bedmen, and all bores:
'At Mrs. Greenland's Hawthorn Bush,' said he,
'I slept.' None knew which bush. Above the town,
Beyond 'The Drover,' a hundred spot the down
In Wiltshire. And where now at last he sleeps
More sound in France—that, too, he secret keeps.

EDWARD THOMAS

AFTERMATH

After the Armistice I waited to hear from him, not daring to ask myself, during those weeks of lively distraction, why no letter arrived. Several months elapsed before I was told about his death. I have never been able to accept that disappearance philosophically. A blank miserable sense of deprivation has dulled my mind whenever I have thought of him, and even now it has needed an effort of will to describe our friendship. Recognition of his poetry has steadily increased; but the chasm in my private existence remains. I am unable to believe that 'whom the gods love die young'.

SIEGFRIED SASSOON on Wilfred Owen[132]

ENVOIE

How shall I say good-bye to you, wonderful, terrible days,
If I should live to live and leave 'neath an alien soil
You, my men, who taught me to walk with a smile in the ways
Of the valley of shadows, taught me to know you and love you, and toil
Glad in the glory of fellowship, happy in misery, strong
In the strength that laughs at its weakness, laughs at its sorrows and
fears,
Facing the world that was not too kind with a jest and a song?
What can the world hold afterwards worthy of laughter or tears?

EDWARD DE STEIN

RETURN

This was the way that, when the war was over,
we were to pass together. You, its lover,
would make me love your land, you said, no less,
its shining levels and their loneliness,
the reedy windings of the silent stream,
your boyhood's playmate, and your childhood's dream.

The war is over now: and we can pass
this way together. Every blade of grass
is you: you are the ripples on the river:
you are the breeze in which they leap and quiver.
I find you in the evening shadows falling
athwart the fen, you in the wildfowl calling:
and all the immanent vision cannot save
my thoughts from wandering to your unknown grave.

E. HILTON YOUNG

KILLED IN ACTION

I his broken-hearted lover?
I his would-be friend of friends?
I who grieve here, brooding over
This of all life's broken ends
Snapped and lost beyond recover—
Who can gather honey from the dark crushed clover?
Who can make amends?

Whose was it to make amending?
Which hand crushed the honeyed bloom?
Yours befriended, or mine befriending?
Nay, but in too little room
Planted we love's seed for tending,
That where skies are endless need have not known ending,
Nor pain nor final gloom.

Half our lives ago, so nearly!
Was it just a childish game?
How could I have loved so dearly,
Friendship prove so fierce a flame?
Yet remembrance answers clearly,
That the changing heart of me in semblance merely
Changeth, still the same.

Aye, the boy's heart, madly burning,
Is the man's heart, scarce aglow.
As spent the sun, seaward returning,
Sinks his reddening bulk below
Long cloud edges past discerning,
Yet we know he shines still, know elsewhere his yearning
Worshippers cry Lo!

Lo, the love I would have given,
Even the love you would not choose,
Now in your unfamiliar heaven
Take and refuse not. You cannot refuse.
Love lives on, though the world be riven.
Love now is master of you. In vain have you striven.
Death doth demand his dues.

GEOFFREY FABER

AFTERMATH

God! this is Death in Life – to wake at morn
Heart-sick with memories; till the sun set
To watch the long day wane, with soul forlorn
For ever striving to forget – forget!
Gone is the old content; from field and flower
The glory fled; Pleasure turned Bitterness;
Desire grown dim ere over the longed-for hour
Might in oblivion steep the heart's distress.

Could I but hear once more the bugle sound,
Into belovéd eyes look once again;
Clasp the strong hand of fighting men—my men,
In one united comradeship firm bound—
From the dead ashes of My Self would soar
A Phoenix-soul in love with Life once more!

F. S. WOODLEY

1916 SEEN FROM 1921

Tired with dull grief, grown old before my day,
I sit in solitude and only hear
Long silent laughters, murmurings of dismay,
The lost intensities of hope and fear;
In those old marshes yet the rifles lie,
On the thin breastwork flutter the grey rags,
The very books I read are there—and I
Dead as the men I loved, wait while life drags

Its wounded length from those sad streets of war
Into green places here, that were my own;
But now what once was mine is mine no more,
I seek such neighbours here and I find none.
With such strong gentleness and tireless will
Those ruined houses seared themselves in me,
Passionate I look for their dumb story still,
And the charred stub outspeaks the living tree.

I rise up at the singing of a bird
And scarcely knowing slink along the lane,
I dare not give a soul a look or word
Where all have homes and none's at home in vain:
Deep red the rose burned in the grim redoubt,
The self-sown wheat around was like a flood,
In the hot path the lizard lolled time out,
The saints in broken shrines were bright as blood.

Sweet Mary's shrine between the sycamores!
There we would go, my friend of friends and I,
And snatch long moments from the grudging wars,
Whose dark made light intense to see them by.
Shrewd bit the morning fog, the whining shots
Spun from the wrangling wire; then in warm swoon
The sun hushed all but the cool orchard plots,
We crept in the tall grass and slept till noon.

EDMUND BLUNDEN

THE MANGEL-BURY

It was after war; Edward Thomas had fallen at Arras—
I was walking by Gloucester musing on such things
As fill his verse with goodness; it was February; the long house
Straw-thatched of the mangels stretched two wide wings;
And looked as part of the earth heaped up by dead soldiers
In the most fitting place – along the hedge's yet-bare lines.
West spring breathed there early, that none foreign divines.
Across the flat country the rattling of the cart sounded;
Heavy of wood, jingling of iron; as he neared me I waited
For the chance perhaps of heaving at those great rounded
Ruddy or orange things – and right to be rolled and hefted
By a body like mine, soldier still, and clean from water.
Silent he assented; till the cart was drifted
High with those creatures, so right in size and matter.
We threw them with our bodies swinging, blood in my ears singing;
His was the thick-set sort of farmer, but well-built –
Perhaps, long before, his blood's name ruled all,
Watched all things for his own. If my luck had so willed
Many questions of lordship I had heard him tell – old
Names, rumours. But my pain to more moving called
And him to some barn business far in the fifteen acre field.

IVOR GURNEY

DICKY BOY AN' ME

You'd never find a thicker pair o' mates than Dick an' me.
  Of course we've 'ad our scraps—just once or twice.
We've bin on share an' share alike for many bloomin' months.
  We shared our blankets (an' we shared our lice).

We 'unted Fritz in couples, we was called 'Them one-eye twins',
  We was reckoned pretty 'ot between the lines.
We used to put the wind up Fritz, but 'ow was 'e to know
  Of the little shivers runnin' down our spines?

And once we went a-courtin' a decent bit of stuff;
  She said my eyes was blue and 'is was brown,
But it really didn't matter, 'cos all four of them was black
  When we'd finished knockin' one another down.

We was out one night a-raidin', and ole Dicky Boy got 'it,
  An' 'e went down with a gaspin' sort o' 'Blast!'
I gets 'im on my shoulders and I starts to make for 'ome,
  And the next I sees is—funnels an' a mast!

I thought I must be balmy, and I takes a look around,
  When some bloke says, 'Drink this and try to sleep.'
But 'longside o' me was Dicky Boy, all white and like a child,
  And me 'eart right up to 'eaven seemed to leap.

Oh, you can keep your Lizzies and your Nellies and your Sals—
  They wouldn't be no good for Dick an' me.
'E's lost 'is leg, I've lost me arm, but we don't give a damn,
  'Cos between us we've a proper kit, you see!

And when we wants a smoke o' nights up gets a pair o' legs.
  'E's got two 'ands to fill the pipes, you see.
We've got our little pension and we've got our little fire,
  An' I've got Dick an' Dicky Boy's got me!

'A TOMMY'

DISABLED

He sat in a wheeled chair, waiting for dark,
And shivered in his ghastly suit of grey,
Legless, sewn short at elbow. Through the park
Voices of boys rang saddening like a hymn,
Voices of play and pleasure after day,
Till gathering sleep had mothered them from him.

* * *

About this time Town used to swing so gay
When glow-lamps budded in the light blue trees,
And girls glanced lovelier as the air grew dim,—
In the old times, before he threw away his knees.
Now he will never feel again how slim
Girls' waists are, or how warm their subtle hands.
All of them touch him like some queer disease.

* * *

There was an artist silly for his face,
For it was younger than his youth, last year.
Now, he is old; his back will never brace;
He's lost his colour very far from here,
Poured it down shell-holes till the veins ran dry,
And half his lifetime lapsed in the hot race
And leap of purple spurted from his thigh.

* * *

One time he liked a blood-smear down his leg,
After the matches, carried shoulder-high.
It was after football, when he'd drunk a peg,
He thought he'd better join.—He wonders why.
Someone had said he'd look a god in kilts,
That's why; and maybe, too, to please his Meg,
Aye, that was it, to please the giddy jilts
He asked to join. He didn't have to beg;
Smiling they wrote his lie: aged nineteen years.
Germans he scarcely thought of; all their guilt,
And Austria's, did not move him. And no fears
Of Fear came yet. He thought of jewelled hilts
For daggers in plaid socks; of smart salutes;
And care of arms; and leave; and pay arrears;
Esprit de corps; and hints for young recruits.
And soon, he was drafted out with drums and cheers.

* * *

Some cheered him home, but not as crowds cheer Goal.
Only a solemn man who brought him fruits
Thanked him; and then enquired about his soul.

* * *

Now, he will spend a few sick years in institutes,
And do what things the rules consider wise,
And take whatever pity they may dole.
Tonight he noticed how the women's eyes
Passed from him to the strong men that were whole.
How cold and late it is! Why don't they come
And put him into bed? Why don't they come?

WILFRED OWEN

FAREWELL

What? to have had gas, and to expect
No more than a week's sick, and to get Blighty—
This is the gods' gift, and not anyway exact
To Ypres, or bad St Julien or Somme Farm.
Don Hancocks, shall I no more see your face frore,
Gloucester-good, in the first light? (But you are dead!)
Shall I see no more Monger with india-rubber
Twisted face? (But machine-gun caught him and his grimace.)
No more to march happy with such good comrades,
Watching the sky, the brown land, the bayonet blades
Moving—to muse on music forgetting the pack.
Nor to hear Gloucester with Stroud debating the lack
Of goodliness or virtue in girls on farmlands.
Nor to hear Cheltenham hurling at Cotswold demands
Of civilization; nor west Severn joking at east Severn?
No more, across the azure or brown lands,
The morning mist of high day clear of rack,
Shall move my dear knees, or feel them frosted, shivering

By Somme or Aubers—or to have a courage from faces
Full of all west England. Her God gives graces.
There was not one of all that battalion
Loved his comrades as well as I—but kept shy.
Or said in verse, what his voice would not rehearse.
So, gassed, I went back to northlands where voices speak soft as in
  verse.
And, after, to meet evil not fit for the thought one touch to dwell on.

Dear battalion, the dead of you would not have let
Your comrade be so long prey for the unquiet
Black evil of the unspoken and concealed pit.
You would have had me safe—dead or free happy alive.

They bruise my head and torture with their own past-hate
Sins of the past, and lie so as earth moves at it.
You dead ones—I lay with you under the unbroken wires once.

IVOR GURNEY

TWO YEARS AFTER

We thought when we sat in the soup, old
  man, with curling flame all round,
We thought if we didn't get scorched or choked
  or buried or boiled or drowned,
We thought to the end of our days on earth
  we should live like kings uncrowned.

We thought if ever we came home alive they
  would fall on our necks half mad,
And turn their hearts for us inside out and load
  us with all they had;
That nothing would be too good for us, since
  nothing was then too bad.

We thought, and the thought of it warmed us
  up, and gave us strength anew,
And carried us on till the task was done; we
  thought—but it wasn't true,
For it isn't much cop down here, old man;
  how is it up there with you?

GEORGE WILLIS

STRANGE HELLS

There are strange hells within the minds war made
Not so often, not so humiliatingly afraid
As one would have expected—the racket and fear guns made.
One hell the Gloucester soldiers they quite put out:
Their first bombardment, when in combined black shout

Of fury, guns aligned, they ducked lower their heads
And sang with diaphragms fixed beyond all dreads,
That tin and stretched-wire tinkle, that blither of tune:
'Après la guerre fini', till hell all had come down,
Twelve-inch, six-inch, and eighteen pounders hammering hell's
  thunders.

Where are they now, on state-doles, or showing shop-patterns
Or walking town to town sore in borrowed tatterns
Or begged. Some civic routine one never learns.
The heart burns—but has to keep out of face how heart burns.

IVOR GURNEY

From 'HUGH SELWYN MAUBERLEY'

These fought in any case,
and some believing,
        pro domo, in any case . . .

Some quick to arm,
some for adventure,
some from fear of weakness,
some from fear of censure,
some for love of slaughter, in imagination,
learning later . . .
some in fear, learning love of slaughter;

Died some, pro patria,
        non 'dulce' non 'et decor' . . .
walked eye-deep in hell
believing in old men's lies, then unbelieving
came home, home to a lie,
home to many deceits,
home to old lies and new infamy;
usury age-old and age-thick
and liars in public places.

Daring as never before, wastage as never before.
Young blood and high blood,
fair cheeks, and fine bodies;

fortitude as never before

frankness as never before,
disillusions as never told in the old days,
hysterias, trench confessions,
laughter out of dead bellies.

* * *

There died a myriad,
And of the best, among them,
For an old bitch gone in the teeth,
For a botched civilization,

Charm, smiling at the good mouth,
Quick eyes gone under earth's lid,

For two gross of broken statues,
For a few thousand battered books.

EZRA POUND

EPILOGUE TO 'DEATH OF A HERO'

Eleven years after the fall of Troy,
We, the old men—some of us nearly forty—
Met and talked on the sunny rampart
Over our wine, while the lizards scuttled
In dusty grass, and the crickets chirred.

Some bared their wounds;
Some spoke of the thirst, dry in the throat,
And the heart-beat, in the din of battle;
Some spoke of intolerable sufferings,
The brightness gone from their eyes
And the grey already thick in their hair.

And I sat a little apart
From the garrulous talk and old memories,
And I heard a boy of twenty
Say petulantly to a girl, seizing her arm:
'Oh, come away, why do you stand there
Listening open-mouthed to the talk of old men?
Haven't you heard enough of Troy and Achilles?
Why should they bore us for ever
With an old quarrel and the names of dead men
We never knew, and dull forgotten battles?'

And he drew her away,
And she looked back and laughed
As he spoke more contempt of us,
Being now out of hearing.
Like the meeting of blade and blade.

And as they two moved further away
He put an arm about her, and kissed her;
And afterwards I heard their gay distant laughter.

And I looked at the hollow cheeks
And the weary eyes and the grey-streaked heads
Of the old men—nearly forty—about me;
And I too walked away
In an agony of helpless grief and pity.

RICHARD ALDINGTON

WAR AND PEACE

In sodden trenches I have heard men speak,
though numb and wretched, wise and witty things;
and loved them for the stubbornness that clings
longest to laughter when Death's pulleys creak;
and seeing cool nurses move on tireless feet
to do abominable things with grace,
dreamed them sweet sisters in that haunted place
where with child voices strong men howl or bleat.

Yet now those men lay stubborn courage by,
riding dull-eyed and silent in the train
to old men's stools; or sell gay-coloured socks
and listen fearfully for Death; so I
love the low-laughing girls, who now again
go daintily, in thin and flowery frocks.

EDGELL RICKWORD

THE WATCHERS

I heard the Challenge 'Who goes there?'
Close kept but mine through midnight air;
I answered and was recognized.
And passed, and kindly thus advised:
'There's someone crawlin' through the grass
By the red ruin, or there was,
And them machine guns been a firin'
All the time the chaps was wirin',
So sir if you're goin' out
You'll keep your 'ead well down no doubt.'

When will the stern fine 'Who goes there?'
Meet me again in midnight air?
And the gruff sentry's kindness, when
Will kindness have such power again?
It seems, as now I wake and brood,
And know my hour's decrepitude,
That on some dewy parapet
The sentry's spirit gazes yet,
Who will not speak with altered tone
When I at last am seen and known.

EDMUND BLUNDEN

LAMENT

We who are left, how shall we look again
Happily on the sun, or feel the rain,
Without remembering how they who went
Ungrudgingly, and spent
Their all for us, loved, too, the sun and rain?

A bird among the rain-wet lilac sings—
But we, how shall we turn to little things
And listen to the birds and winds and streams
Made holy by their dreams,
Nor feel the heart-break in the heart of things?

WILFRED GIBSON

TWO FUSILIERS

And have we done with War at last?
Well, we've been lucky devils both,
And there's no need of pledge or oath
To bind our lovely friendship fast,
By firmer stuff
Close bound enough.

By wire and wood and stake we're bound,
By Fricourt and by Festubert,
By whipping rain, by the sun's glare,
By all the misery and loud sound,
By a Spring day,
By Picard clay.

Show me the two so closely bound
As we, by the wet bond of blood,
By friendship, blossoming from mud,
By Death: we faced him, and we found
Beauty in Death,
In dead men breath.

ROBERT GRAVES

ENVOI

REALITY

Below my room the noise and measured beat
Of marching men re-echoed loud and clear;
Now bobbing cavalry swung down the street;
Now mules and rumbling batteries drew near.
But all is dim—The rolling wagon-stream
To Amiens between the aspen trees,
The stables, billets, men and horses, seem
Dead mummers of forgotten fantasies.

Only my dreams are still aglow, a throng
Of scenes that crowded through a waiting mind.
A myriad scenes: For I have swept along
To foam ashriek with gulls, and rowed behind
Brown oarsmen swinging to an ocean song
Where stately galleons bowed before the wind.

GEOFFREY DEARMER

NOTES

1 Paul Fussell, *The Great War and Modern Memory*, London, OUP, 1975, p 279–280.
2 John Ellis, *Eye-deep in Hell*, London, Croom Helm, 1976, p 197.
3 W. T. Stead to Edward Carpenter, letter in *Edward Carpenter Collection*, Sheffield City Libraries, June 1895, MS 386–54 (1–2).
4 *Great War*, p 272.
5 Siegfried Sassoon, *Diaries 1915–1918*, edited and introduced by Rupert Hart-Davis, London, Faber, 1983, p 9.
6 Siegfried Sassoon, *Sherston's Progress*, London, Faber, 1937, p 214.
7 *Diaries* 1915–1918, p 262.
8 Quoted in P. N. Furbank, *E. M. Forster: a life* (Volume II), Oxford, OUP, 1979, p 55.
9 *Diaries 1915–1918*, p 216.
10 ibid, p 242.
11 Arthur Graeme West, *The Diary of a Dead Officer*, London, Allen & Unwin, 1918, p 80.
12 Eleanor Farjeon, *Edward Thomas: the last four years*, London, OUP, 1958, p 154.
13 Wilfred Owen, *Collected Letters*, edited by Harold Owen and John Bell, London, OUP, p 571; ibid, p 570.
14 ibid, p 586.
15 *Diary of a Dead Officer*, p 79.
16 *Diaries 1915–1918*, p 121.
17 Peter Austen, *The Young Gods*, Sydney, Tyrrel's Limited, 1919, p 11.
18 Frederic Manning, *The Middle Parts of Fortune*, London, Peter Davies, 1929, p 377.
19 Quoted in *Eye-deep in Hell*, p 200.
20 Henry Williamson, *A Patriot's Progress*, London, Geoffrey Bles, 1930, p 117.
21 C. E. Montague, *Disenchantment*, London, Chatto & Windus, 1922, p 35.

22 ibid, p 36.
23 Herbert Read, *The Contrary Experience*, London, Secker & Warburg, 1963, p 97.
24 Quoted in *Eye-deep in Hell*, p 199.
25 *Disenchantment*, p 36.
26 H. L. Simpson, *Moods and Tenses*, London, Erskine Macdonald, 1919, p 10.
27 Quoted in *Eye-deep in Hell*, p 198.
28 *Middle Parts*, p 114.
29 ibid, p 27.
30 J. B. Priestley, *Margin Released: A Writer's Reminiscences and Reflections*, London, Heinemann, 1962, p 89.
31 R. E. Vernède, *War Poems*, London, Heinemann, 1917, p 27.
32 H. O. Sturgis, *Tim*, London, Macmillan, 1891; J. E. C. Welldon, *Gerald Eversley's Friendship*, London, Smith & Co, 1896; H. A. Vachell, *The Hill*, London, John Murray, 1905; E. F. Benson, *David Blaize*, London, Hodder & Stoughton, 1916.
33 *Moods and Tenses*, p 6.
34 Robert Graves, *Goodbye to All That*, London, Jonathan Cape, 1929, p 40–41.
35 *Diaries 1915–1918*, p 44–45.
36 Eric Hiscock, *The Bells of Hell go Ting-a-ling-a-ling*, London, Arlington Books, 1976, p 35–36.
37 ibid, p 25; ibid, p 36.
38 ibid, p 97–98.
39 John Jolliffe, *Raymond Asquith: Life and Letters*, London, Collins, 1980, p 292.
40 J. R. Ackerley, *My Father and Myself*, London, Bodley Head, 1968, p 117.
41 Richard Aldington, *Death of a Hero*, London, Chatto & Windus, 1929, p 26.
42 *My Father*, p 119.
43 Robert Graves, *But it Still Goes on*, London, Jonathan Cape, 1930, p 245.
44 Charles Carrington, *Soldier From the Wars Returning*, London, Heinemann, 1965, p 219.

45 J. R. Ackerley, *The Prisoners of War*, London, Chatto & Windus, 1925, p 86.
46 ibid, p 91.
47 Quoted in Diana Cooper, *The Rainbow Comes and Goes*, London, Rupert Hart-Davis, 1959, p 160.
48 Robert Graves, *Difficult Questions, Easy Answers*, London, Cassell, 1972, p 183.
49 T. E. Lawrence, *Seven Pillars of Wisdom*, London, Jonathan Cape, London, 1940, p 28.
50 Quoted in Phillip Knightley and Colin Simpson, *The Secret Lives of Lawrence of Arabia*, London, Nelson, 1969, p 155.
51 *Seven Pillars*, p 454.
52 Quoted in Martin Seymour-Smith, *Robert Graves: His Life and Work*, London, Hutchinson, 1982, p 21; *Goodbye*, p 220.
53 Robert Graves, *Over the Brazier*, London, Poetry Bookshop, 1916, p 16.
54 Graves wrote in 1943: 'Owen was a weakling, really; I liked him but there was that passive homosexual streak in him which is even more disgusting than that active one in Auden.' Quoted in *Robert Graves*, p 63.
55 James S. Yates, *War Lyrics*, Oxford, Blackwell, 1919, p 67.
56 Herbert Read, 'Foreword', *Promise of Greatness*, edited by George Panichas, London, Cassell, 1968, p vi.
57 Maurice Baring, *Poems: 1914–1917*, London, Martin Secker, 1918, p 11.
58 Brian Reade, *Sexual Heretics*, London, Routledge & Kegan Paul, 1970, p 9.
59 *Bells of Hell*, p. 98.
60 T. S. Eliot, *Collected Poems 1909–1962*, London, Faber, 1963, p 75.
61 Quoted in M. van Wyck Smith, *Drummer Hodge: the Poetry of the Anglo-Boer War* (1899–1902), Oxford, OUP, 1978, p 198.
62 ibid, p 198.
63 Correlli Barnett, *Britain and her Army 1509–1970*, London, Allen Lane, 1970, p 139.
64 Rudyard Kipling, *Departmental Ditties and Barrack-Room Ballads*, London, Review of Reviews, 1915, p 149.
65 ibid, p 148.

66 Quoted in Guy Arnold, *Hold Fast for England: G. A. Henty, Imperialist Boy's Writer*, London, Hamish Hamilton, 1980, p 63.
67 Quoted in ibid, p 22.
68 Charles Carrington, *Kipling: His Life and Work*, London, Macmillan, 1955, p 105.
69 Rudyard Kipling, *Twenty Poems*, London, Methuen, 1918, p 10.
70 A. E. Housman, 'The Isle of Portland', *A Shropshire Lad*, London, Grant Richards, 1914, p 88.
71 ibid, p 33–34.
72 David Jones, *In Parenthesis*, London, Faber, 1937, p 221.
73 *Great War*, p 282.
74 Quoted in *Robert Graves*, p 469.
75 *An Anthology of War Poetry*, edited by Robert Nichols, London, Nicholson & Watson, 1943, p 29.
76 *Sexual Heretics*, p 48–49.
77 *Great War*, p 284.
78 Geoffrey Faber, *The Buried Stream*, London, Faber, 1941, p 207.
79 *Great War*, p 284–285.
80 *My Father*, p 115.
81 *Bells of Hell*, p 143.
82 Hugh Reginald Freston, *The Quest of Truth*, Oxford, Blackwell, 1916, p 49.
83 *Bells of Hell*, p 145.
84 Peter Parker, *The Old Lie: the Great War and the Public School Ethos*, London, Constable, 1987, p 188.
85 Quoted in Geoffrey Palmer and Noel Lloyd, *E. F. Benson: as he was*, London, Lennard Publishing, 1988, p 102.
86 Edward Carpenter, *Towards Democracy*, Manchester, John Heywood, 1883, p 75.
87 Walt Whitman, 'I hear it was charged against me', *Leaves of Grass*, New York, New English Library, 1955, p 123.
88 Isaac Rosenberg, *Collected Works*, edited with an introduction by Ian Parsons, London, Chatto & Windus, 1979, p 248.
89 ibid, p 111.
90 Siegfried Sassoon, 'Song', *A Private Anthology*, made by N. G. Royde-Smith, London, Constable, 1924, p 79.

91 Siegfried Sassoon, *The War Poems*, arranged and introduced by Rupert Hart-Davis, London, Faber, 1983, p 69.
92 Quoted in *Sexual Heretics*, p 20.
93 Oscar Wilde, *Collected Works*, edited by G. F. Maine, London, Collins, 1948, p 90.
94 Charles Carrington, 'Some soldiers', *Promise of Greatness*, p 157.
95 Siegfried Sassoon, *Memoirs of an Infantry Officer*, London, Faber, 1930, p 241.
96 Paul Delaney, *The Neo-Pagans: Friendship and Love in the Rupert Brooke Circle*, London, Macmillan, 1987, p 209.
97 Robert Nichols, 'The Past', *Ardours and Endurances*, London, Chatto & Windus, 1917, p 5.
98 Wilfred Owen, *Collected Poems*, edited with an introduction and notes by C. Day-Lewis, London, Chatto & Windus, 1963, p 113.
99 Dominic Hibberd, *Owen the Poet*, London, Macmillan, 1987, p 68.
100 *Sexual Heretics*, p 145.
101 Quoted in *Owen the Poet*, p 155.
102 *Collected Letters*, p 112.
103 Bernard Bergonzi, *Heroes Twilight*, London, Constable, 1965, p 128.
104 *Collected Letters*, p 580.
105 *Prisoners*, p 68.
106 C. Day-Lewis, *A Hope for Poetry*, Oxford, Peters & Co, 1934, p 18.
107 *Goodbye*, p 285.
108 Ivor Novello and L. G. Ford, *Keep the Home Fires Burning*, London, Ascherberg, Hopwood & Crew, 1914.
109 *Goodbye*, p 283.
110 *Diaries 1915–1918*, p 275.
111 *Infantry Officer*, p 215.
112 ibid, p 89.
113 ibid, p 290.
114 *War Returning*, p 252–253.
115 Ivor Gurney, 'After "The Penny Whistle"', *Collected Poems*, chosen, edited and with an introduction by P. J. Kavanagh, Oxford, OUP, 1982, p 158.
116 Edmund Blunden, *Undertones of War*, London, R. Cobden-Sanderson, 1928, p 154.

117 *Diaries 1915–1918*, p 94.
118 Siegfried Sassoon, *Diaries 1920–1922*, edited and introduced by Rupert Hart-Davis, London, Faber, 1981, p 73–74.
119 *Margin Released*, p 89.
120 *Collected Letters*, p 596.
121 Charles Carrington ('Charles Edmonds'), *A Subaltern's War*, London, Peter Davies, 1922, p 200.
122 Quoted in *Great War*, p 280.
123 *Anthology of War Poetry*, p 34.
124 Ivor Gurney, *War Letters*, a selection edited by R. K. R. Thornton, London, Hogarth Press, 1984, p 67.
125 *Collected Letters*, p 581.
126 *War Letters*, p 225–226.
127 *Diaries 1915–1918*, p 22.
128 *War Letters*, p 106.
129 *Promise of Greatness*, p 164.
130 *Diaries 1915–1918*, p 45.
131 *Collected Letters*, p 591.
132 Siegfried Sassoon, *Siegfried's Journey*, London, Faber, 1946, p 72.

BIOGRAPHICAL NOTES

Richard Aldington (1892–1962)
Born Edward Godfree Aldington in Hampshire, and educated at Dover College and University of London. One of the founders of Imagism in 1912 with his future wife Hilda Doolittle and Ezra Pound, and editor of the house magazine *Egoist*. Volunteered in 1914 but rejected on medical grounds until May 1916. Served in France from November 1916, initially in the ranks of 8th Battalion, Devonshire Regiment and 8th Battalion, Royal Sussex Regiment. Commissioned in November 1917 as a 2nd Lieutenant in 9th Battalion, Royal Sussex Regiment. Severely gassed and shell-shocked in 1918, and demobilized in January 1919. War experiences are covered in fiction in *Death of a Hero* (1929) and *Roads to Glory* (1930): and autobiography *Life for Life's Sake* (1941). War poems appear in *Images* (1919), *Images of War* (1919) and *Complete Poems* (1948). After the war wrote several novels and volumes of poetry, critical works on French literature and contentious biographies of D. H. Lawrence and T. E. Lawrence.

Philip Gillespie Bainbrigge (1891–1918)
Born in London, and educated at Eton and Trinity College, Cambridge. Master at Shrewsbury School September 1913–March 1917. After training with Inns of Court OTC from May 1917, commissioned in November 1917 as a 2nd Lieutenant in 4th Battalion, Lancashire Fusiliers, although served with 15th Battalion, Welsh Regiment in France from February 1918. Killed in action at Battle of Epèhy on 18 September 1918. His one war poem, a scurrilous response to Brooke, appeared in *Slide Rule* (1954), the autobiography of Nevil Shute, a former pupil. His witty Uranian play *Achilles in Scyros* is quoted in *Love in Earnest*. Wilfred Owen met Bainbrigge at Scarborough in February 1918 and thought well enough of him to slate him for a copy of his projected *Poems*.

Frederick William Duffield Bendall (1882–1953)
Born in Manningtree, Essex, and educated at Ipswich School and Selwyn College, Cambridge. Served with Territorial Force from 1910 in 3rd Battalion (Royal Fusiliers), London Regiment. Promoted to Lieutenant-Colonel in September 1914 and appointed to raise and command 2/3rd Battalion (Royal Fusiliers), London Regiment. Served in Malta December 1914–April 1915, Sudan April 1915–August 1915 (OC British troops at Khartoum) and Gallipoli September 1915. Invalided home with frostbite in January 1916. Served in France July 1916–May 1918 commanding 8th Battalion, Middlesex Regiment. Awarded Mention in Despatches twice in 1917 and CMG in January 1918. Wounded in 1918 and passed for Home Service in May 1918. Relinquished commission through ill-health in April 1919. Re-gazetted to Unattached List (TF) to command Bridlington School OTC in May 1919. After the war worked for inspectorate of Board (later Ministry) of Education. Served as Director of Army Education 1940–1942. War poems appear in *Front Line Lyrics* (1918).

Edmund Charles Blunden (1896–1974)
Born in London, educated at Christ's Hospital and after the war at Queen's College, Cambridge. Enlisted in 1914 and commissioned in September 1915 as a 2nd Lieutenant in 10th Battalion, Royal Sussex Regiment. Served in France with 11th Battalion, Royal Sussex Regiment spring 1916–early 1919. Awarded MC in November 1916 and promoted to Lieutenant in September 1917. After the war worked for *Athenæum* and *Nation* 1920–1924, became Professor of English at Tokyo University 1924–1927 and a fellow of Merton College, Oxford 1931–1943. Ran courses in map-reading for London University OTC in Second World War and joined staff of *Times Literary Supplement* in 1943. Later with UK Liaision Mission to Tokyo 1948–1950 and Professor of Poetry at Oxford 1966–1968. Respected poet and critic, editor of Owen and Gurney and champion of First World War poetry, other than his own. Friend of Sassoon. War experiences covered in *Undertones of War* (1928), which includes some war poems, and *The Mind's Eye* (1934). War poems also appear in *The Shepherd, And Other Poems of Peace and War* (1922), *Masks of Time* (1925) and collected edition *Poems 1914–1930* (1930).

'Harry Brander'
This was the pseudonym used by Eva Mudocci. The war poems appear in *For Them: Poems and Anecdotes of the War* (1934).

Rupert Chawner Brooke (1887–1915)
Born and educated at Rugby, where his father was a housemaster, and King's College, Cambridge. Leading light of Georgian movement and member of Fabian circle. First volume of verse *Poems 1911* (1911) criticized for being too realistic. Enlisted in August 1914 as a Sub-Lieutenant in Royal Naval Division. Served with Anson Battalion in the retreat from Antwerp in October 1914. *1914* sonnets sprang from this experience and fed previously lukewarm appetite for war. Sailed for Gallipoli with Hood Battalion, Royal Naval Division, but died of blood-poisoning en route on 23 April 1915 and buried on island of Skyros. War poems appear in *1914: and Other Poems* (1915) and *Collected Poems* (1918).

John Lewis Crommelin Brown
Educated at Trinity College, Cambridge. Master at Repton School. After training with Cadet School at Trowbridge commissioned as a 2nd Lieutenant in Royal Garrison Artillery (Special Reserve) in December 1915. In France from February 1916. Shell-shocked and invalided home in March 1916. Instructor at Cadet School, Trowbridge May 1917–July 1918. Promoted to Lieutenant in July 1917. Served in Salonika August 1918–May 1919 and demobilized in June 1919. War poems appear in *Dies Heroica: War Poems: 1914–1918* (1918).

Arthur Newberry Choyce (b. 1897)
Commissioned in December 1916 as a 2nd Lieutenant in 9th Battalion, Leicestershire Regiment. Promoted to Lieutenant in July 1917. Served in France 1917–1918. Wrote verse after the war. War poems appear in *Crimson Stains* (1917) and *Memory* (1918).

Edward Sinauer de Stein (1887–1965)
Educated at Eton and Magdalen College, Oxford. Served with Oxford University OTC from before the outbreak of war, and in March 1915 attached as a Captain to 11th Battalion, Kings Royal Rifle Corps. Went to France in July 1915 and transferred to Machine Gun Corps in October 1915. Promoted to Major in February 1918. After the war became important figure in commercial and financial worlds. Knighted in 1946 for his work with Ministry

of Supply from 1941. War poems appear in *Poets in Picardy, and Other Poems* (1919).

Geoffrey Dearmer (b 1893)
Born in Lambeth, and educated at Westminster and Christ's College, Oxford. Commissioned in September 1914 as a 2nd Lieutenant in 2/2nd Battalion (Royal Fusiliers), London Regiment. Promoted to Lieutenant in November 1914. Served in Malta December 1914–August 1915, Gallipoli September 1915–January 1916 and Egypt January–April 1916. Attached to 1/2nd Battalion (Royal Fusiliers), London Regiment in France, in June 1916. Transferred to Royal Army Service Corps in August 1916, and mentioned by Secretary of State for valuable war services in August 1919. After the war published several volumes of poetry, novels and plays. Appointed Examiner of Plays to Lord Chamberlain 1936–1958 and editor of 'Children's Hour', BBC 1939–1959. War poems appear in *Poems* (1918) and *The Day's Delight* (1923).

Richard Molesworth Dennys (1884–1916)
Born in Kensington, and educated at Winchester College and St Bartholomew's Hospital, London. Eschewed medical career to study theatre design with Gordon Craig in Florence. Returned to England at outbreak of war and commissioned in September 1914 as a 2nd Lieutenant in 10th Battalion, Loyal North Lancashire Regiment. Promoted to Temporary Lieutenant in October 1914 and to Temporary Captain in December 1914. Served in France from August 1915. Died of wounds in hospital at Rouen on 24 July 1916 from injuries sustained on 12 July during the Somme advance. War poems appear in *There is no Death* (1917).

Godfrey Elton (1892–1973)
Born in Sherington, near Newport Pagnell, and educated at Rugby, and Balliol and Queen's College, Oxford. Commissioned in September 1914 as a 2nd Lieutenant in 2/4th Battalion, Hampshire Regiment. Served in India November 1914–October 1915, transferred to 1/4th Battalion and served in Mesopotamia October 1915–April 1916. Promoted to Lieutenant in January 1916. Wounded and captured at Kut al Amara, marched to Kastamuni in Turkey and held as a prisoner of war from June 1916. Repatriated in December 1918 and promoted to Captain in January 1919. After the war, lecturer in Modern History at Queen's College, Oxford 1919–1939. Labour

candidate for Thornbury District 1924 and 1929, and expelled from Labour Party in September 1931 as a supporter of Ramsay MacDonald. Editor of National Labour Committee newsletter 1931–1937. Became 1st Baron Elton in 1934 and General Secretary of Rhodes Trust 1939–1959. Novelist and historical essayist, and active on many civic committees. Friend of Sassoon. War experiences covered in *Among Others* (1938). War poems appear in *Schoolboys and Exiles* (1919) and *Years of Peace* (1925).

Geoffrey Cust Faber (1889–1961)
Born in Malvern, and educated at Rugby and Christ's Church and All Souls, Oxford. Commissioned as a 2nd Lieutenant in November 1914 and attached to 3rd Glamorgan Battery, Royal Field Artillery (TF). Transferred to 2/8th Battalion (Post Office Rifles), London Regiment in February 1915. Promoted to Temporary Lieutenant in September 1915 and to Captain in March 1917. Served in France January–March 1917 and April 1918–early 1919. After the war became founder and first president of Faber and Faber Ltd and president of Council of Publishers Association. Knighted in 1954. War poems appear in *Interflow* (1915), *In the Valley of Vision* (1918) and *The Buried Stream* (1941).

James Griffyth Fairfax (1886–1976)
Born in Sydney, educated at Winchester and New College, Oxford and served with Oxford University OTC. First volume of poetry appeared in 1908. Commissioned in December 1914 as a 2nd Lieutenant in Army Service Corps. Promoted to Lieutenant in August 1915 and attached to 15th Indian Divisional Train in May 1916. Served in Mesopotamia 1917–1919. Promoted to Captain in May 1918 and awarded Mention in Despatches in 1917, 1918 (twice) and 1919. After the war practised law in Australia, then returned to England and became Conservative MP for Norwich 1924–1929. Poet, translator and journalist. War poems appear in *The Temple of Janus* (1917) and *Mesopotamia* (1919).

Frank Stewart Flint (1885–1960)
Born in Islington, left school at 13, joined Civil Service as a typist at 19, and studied Latin and French at night school. Became a leading member of the Imagists, and friend of T. E. Hulme, Ezra Pound and Richard Aldington (to whom 'Soldiers' is dedicated). Served in the ranks in England with 25th Battalion, Rifle Brigade 1917–1919. After the war worked for Ministry of Labour and became Chief of Overseas Section, Statistics Division, retiring in

1950. Translator, notable critic of French literature and reviewer. War poems appear in last volume of verse *Otherworld: Cadences* (1920).

Gilbert Frankau (1884–1952)
Born in London, educated at Eton, worked in family tobacco business from 1904 and travelled the world 1912–1914. Commissioned in October 1914 as a 2nd Lieutenant in 9th Battalion, East Surrey Regiment. Transferred to Royal Field Artillery in March 1915 and went to France. In October 1916 appointed staff captain for special propaganda duties in Italy. Promoted to Captain in November 1917 and invalided out of service with delayed shell-shock in February 1918. Re-commissioned in August 1939 in RAF Volunteer Reserve, promoted to Squadron Leader in April 1940 and invalided out of service in February 1941. Prolific author of verse, novels and non-fiction. War experiences covered in novel *Peter Jackson, Cigar Merchant* (1919). War poems appear in *The Guns* (1916), *The City of Fear* (1917), *The Other Side* (1918), *The Judgement of Valhalla* (1918) and *Collected Poems* (1923).

Hugh Reginald 'Rex' Freston (1891–1916)
Born at Tulse Hill, and educated at Dulwich College and Exeter College, Oxford. At outbreak of war joined Oxford University OTC and commissioned in April 1915 as a 2nd Lieutenant in 3rd Battalion, Royal Berkshire Regiment. Transferred to 6th Battalion and went to France in December 1915. Killed in action on 24 January 1916 at La Boiselle. War poems appear in *The Quest of Beauty* (1915) and *The Quest of Truth* (1916). Friend of Robert Nichols.

Wilfred Wilson Gibson (1878–1958)
Born in Hexham, Northumberland. Received no formal education, but became full-time poet with publication of first volume in 1902. Leading member of Georgian group, and friend of Brooke, Thomas, Harold Monro, Lascelles Abercrombie and John Drinkwater. Volunteered in 1915 but rejected four times due to poor eyesight. Eventually enlisted in 1917 and served with Royal Army Service Corps in England. After the war continued to publish poetry, and as a legatee of Brooke's will was assured a regular income. War poems appear in *Battle* (1915), *Friends* (1916), *Livelihood* (1917), *Whin* (1918) and *Neighbours* (1920).

Louis Golding (1895–1958)
Born in Manchester, and educated at Manchester Grammar School and, after the war, Queen's College, Oxford. Unfit for combatant service, but served with Friends' Ambulance Unit in Salonika and France 1914–1919. Became prolific novelist, essayist and travel-writer. War poems appear in *Sorrows of War* (1919) and *Shepherd Singing Ragtime, and Other Poems* (1921).

Robert Graves (1895–1985)
Born in London, and educated at Charterhouse and, after the war, St John's College, Oxford. Commissioned in August 1914 as a 2nd Lieutenant in 3rd Battalion, Royal Welch Fusiliers. Served France April 1915–July 1916, initially with 2nd Battalion, Welsh Regiment April–July 1915, then 2nd Battalion, Royal Welch Fusiliers July–November 1915, then 1st Battalion November 1915–July 1916. Promoted to Lieutenant in May 1915 and to Captain in October 1915. Wounded in July 1916 and after convalescence in England returned to France January–February 1917. Ill-health prevented further active service and posted for home duties until demobilization in February 1919. After the war became Professor of English Literature at Cairo University 1925–1927 and later Professor of Poetry at Oxford 1961–1966. Friend of Sassoon, Owen, Blunden and T. E. Lawrence. Distinguished poet, novelist, critic and mythologrpher. War experiences covered in *Goodbye to All That* (1929) and *But it Still Goes on* (1930). War poems appear in *Over the Brazier* (1916), *Goliath and David* (1917), *Fairies and Fusiliers* (1917), *Country Sentiment* (1920) and *Poems about War* (1988).

R. D. Greenway
Educated at Magdalen College, Oxford. Commissioned in April 1915 as a 2nd Lieutenant in 10th Battalion, Rifle Brigade. Transferred to 7th Battalion in August 1915 and served in France 1915–1917. Transferred to 5th Battalion in May 1917 and promoted to Lieutenant in July 1917. Attached to 4th Battalion in March 1918 and served in Salonika and Serbia 1918–1919. War poems appear in *Moods* (1917).

Ivor Gurney (1890–1937)
Born in Gloucester, and educated at King's School, Gloucester and Royal College of Music. Volunteered in August 1914 but rejected due to defective eyesight. Enlisted in February 1915 as a Private in 2/5th Battalion,

Gloucestershire Regiment. Served in France May 1915–September 1917, when gassed and invalided home. Symptoms of mental instability had appeared before the war but from November 1917 became pronounced. Discharged from army in October 1918 with delayed shell-shock. After several years of aimless wandering, although producing some of his best music and verse, was committed to an asylum in October 1922 with paranoid schizophrenia. Remained institutionalized until death in December 1937. Although the war did not cause his madness, it aggravated his instability into a chronic condition. War experiences are covered in *War Letters* (1983). War poems appear in *Severn and Somme* (1917), *War's Embers* (1919) and *Collected Poems* (1982).

Thomas Hardy (1840–1920)
Born in Brockhampton, Dorset. Trained as an architect, but turned to literature, producing first novel in 1871 and first volume of verse in 1898. As author of *Poems of the Past and the Present* (1901) and *The Dynasts* (1903–1908) Hardy was a war poet before the outbreak of the First World War, an event anticipated in *Satires of Circumstance* (1914). War poems appear in *Moments of Vision* (1917) and *Late Lyrics and Earlier* (1922).

Alan Patrick Herbert (1890–1971)
Born in Elstead, Surrey, and educated at Winchester and New College, Oxford. Enlisted in August 1914 as an Ordinary Seaman in Benbow Battalion, Royal Naval Division. Commissioned in March 1915 as a Sub-Lieutenant in Hawke Battalion, Royal Naval Division. Served in Gallipoli from May 1915 and awarded Mention in Despatches. After garrison duty at Imbros January–May 1916, sent to France with Division. Wounded at Gavrelle in April 1917 and invalided home. Promoted to Lieutenant in September 1917 and subsequently served on staff of HMS *President*. After the war worked for *Punch* from 1924 and wrote many books and plays. Became Independent MP for Oxford University 1935–50 and knighted in 1945. During Second World War served with River Emergency Service on Thames from September 1939 and as a Petty Officer in Naval Auxiliary Patrol from June 1940. First World War experiences covered in the novel *The Secret Battle* (1919) and autobiography *A.P.H. His Life and Times* (1970). War poems appear in *Half-hours at Helles* (1916) and *The Bomber Gypsy, and Other Poems* (1918).

Raymond Heywood
Served as a Lieutenant in France, Macedonia and Salonika, probably with 10th Battalion, Devonshire Regiment. Name is presumably a pseudonym as no such officer appears in Army Lists. War poems appear in *Roses, Pearls and Tears* (1918) and *The Greater Love: Poems of Remembrance* (1919).

William Noel Hodgson (1893–1916)
Born in Petersfield, Hampshire, and educated at Durham School and Christ Church, Oxford. Commissioned in September 1914 as a 2nd Lieutenant in 9th Battalion, Devonshire Regiment. Went to France in July 1915 and promoted to Lieutenant in September 1915. Awarded Mention in Despatches and MC in October 1915. Killed in action on 1 July 1916 in the Battle of the Somme. War poems appear in *Verse and Prose in Peace and War* (1916).

David Jones (1895–1974)
Born in Brockley, Kent, and studied at Camberwell and Westminster Schools of Art. Enlisted in 1915 as a Private in 15th Battalion, Royal Welch Fusiliers. Served in France until 1918 when wounded and invalided home. After the war worked with Eric Gill at Ditchling, and became leading illustrator and watercolourist. Wrote *In Parenthesis* (1937) after a nervous breakdown. Awarded Hawthornden Prize in 1938.

Geoffrey Anketell Studdert Kennedy (1883–1929)
Born in Leeds, and educated at Leeds Grammar School and Trinity College, Dublin. Ordained as an Anglican minister in 1908 and became an army chaplain in December 1915. Served in France 1916–1918. Known as 'Woodbine Willie' for his ready supply of cigarettes, and popular among troops for this and his willingness to share their hardships. After the war continued to write poetry and to champion the underprivileged. War poems appear in *Rough Rhymes of a Padre* (1918), *More Rough Rhymes of a Padre* (1920) and *The Unutterable Beauty* (1927).

Thomas Edward Lawrence (1888–1935)
Born at Tremadoc, Caernarvonshire. Educated at Oxford High School and Jesus and Magdalen Colleges, Oxford. In October 1914 joined Military Intelligence and served in Egypt and Arabia 1914–1918 with rank of Colonel.

Awarded Mention in Despatches for services in Egypt in 1915 and at Hejaz in 1918. Also awarded CB and DSO in 1918, but later refused these in protest at treatment of Arabs after the war. Elected Fellow of All Souls in November 1919. Worked for Middle East Department of Colonial Office 1921–1922. Served in ranks of RAF August 1922–January 1923, Tank Corps March 1923–August 1925 and RAF August 1925–February 1935. Posted to India 1926–1929. Died from injuries sustained in a road accident on 19 May 1935. 'To S.A.' appears as a preface to *Seven Pillars of Wisdom* (1926).

Joseph Johnston Lee (1879–1954)
Born in Dundee, and studied at Heatherly's and the Slade. Enlisted in 1914 in the ranks of 1/4th Battalion, Black Watch and went to France in February 1915. Commissioned in August 1917 as a 2nd Lieutenant in 10th Battalion, King's Royal Rifle Corps. Taken prisoner in November 1917 and repatriated in January 1919. After the war became a professional artist. POW experiences covered in *Captive at Carlsruhe* (1920). War poems appear in *Ballads of Battle* (1916) and *Work-a-day Warriors* (1917).

Walter Scott Stuart Lyon (1886–1915)
Born in North Berwick, and educated at Haileybury and Balliol College, Oxford. Served in 9th Battalion, Royal Scots (Territorial Force), with rank of Lieutenant from December 1912. Mobilized in August 1914 and went to France in February 1915. Killed in action on 8 May 1915 in Second Battle of Ypres. War poems appear in *Easter at Ypres, 1915, and Other Poems* (1916).

Murray McClymont
Commissioned in March 1917 as a 2nd Lieutenant in 2/10th Battalion, King's (Liverpool Regiment) and promoted to Lieutenant in September 1918. Met Wilfred Owen in September 1918 at Étaples and gave him an inscribed copy of *Soldier Poets*. Served with 10th Battalion until late 1921. Wrote several plays in the 'Thirties. War poems appear in anthology *Soldier Poets: More Songs by Fighting Men* (1917).

Patrick MacGill (b. 1890)
Born in Donegal, received no formal education and worked as a labourer between the ages of 12 and 19. Joined editorial staff of *Daily Express* in 1911. Enlisted at outbreak of war and became a Sergeant in 1/18th Battalion

(London Irish Rifles), London Regiment. Went to France in March 1915 and wounded at Loos in October 1915. After the war became prolific author. War experiences covered in *The Amateur Army* (1915), *The Red Horizon* (1916) and *The Great Push* (1916). War poems appear in *Soldier Songs* (1916).

Ewart Alan Mackintosh (1893–1917)
Born at Brighton, and educated at St Paul's and Christ Church, Oxford. Commissioned in December 1914 as a 2nd Lieutenant in 5th Battalion, Seaforth Highlanders, went to France in July 1915 and promoted to Lieutenant in December 1915. Awarded MC in May 1916, wounded and gassed at High Wood in August 1916 and invalided home. Trained cadets in Cambridge, posted to 4th Battalion, Seaforth Highlanders in France in October 1917 and killed in action at Cambrai on 21 November 1917. War poems appear in *A Highland Regiment* (1917) and *War, the Liberator, and Other Pieces* (1918).

Frederic Manning (1887–1935)
Born and educated in Australia, and came to England to work as a writer and critic, publishing first book of poems in 1907. Enlisted in 1915 as a Private in 7th Battalion, King's Shropshire Regiment. Served in France 1915–1917. Commissioned in May 1917 as a 2nd Lieutenant in 6th Battalion, Royal Irish Regiment, but poor health prevented further active service and demobilized in March 1918. After war became great friend of T. E. Lawrence. War experiences covered in novel *The Middle Parts of Fortune* (1929), thought by many to be the finest war novel. War poems appear in *Eidola* (1917).

Richard Brereton Marriott-Watson (d. 1918)
Commissioned in December 1914 as a 2nd Lieutenant in 8th Battalion, East Lancashire Regiment and later attached to 10th Battalion. Transferred to 13th Battalion, Royal Irish Rifles in September 1915 and went to France in October. Attached to 2nd Battalion from May 1916 and awarded MC later that year. Promoted to Lieutenant in November 1917. Killed in action at Cugny on 24 March 1918 while serving with 1st Battalion. War poem first appeared in the *Observer* in 1918.

Harold Monro (1879–1932)
Born in Brussels, and educated at Radley and Caius College, Cambridge.

First volume of poetry published in 1906. Opened Poetry Bookshop in 1913 and with Edward Marsh published all five volumes of *Georgian Poetry* from there. Many of the Georgians, including Brooke and Gibson, were visitors, as were T. E. Hulme, Owen, Thomas, Osbert Sitwell, Isaac Rosenberg, Godfrey Elton and Joseph Leftwich. Unfit for overseas service, but commissioned in June 1916 as a 2nd Lieutenant in Royal Garrison Artillery and served with an anti-aircraft battery. Transferred to War Office in 1917. War poems appear in *Children of Love* (1914) and *Strange Meetings* (1917).

Robert Malise Bowyer Nichols (1893–1944)
Born in Shanklin, Isle of Wight, and educated at Winchester and Trinity College, Oxford. Commissioned in October 1914 as a 2nd Lieutenant in 104th Brigade, Royal Field Artillery. Went to France in August 1915 but by August 1916 invalided out with shell-shock. In 1918 part of British Mission (Ministry of Information) to USA, giving lectures on war poetry. Friend of Graves, Sassoon and the Sitwells. After the war Professor of English Literature, Tokyo University 1921–1924. Poet and playwright. War poems appear in *Invocation* (1915), *Ardours and Endurances* (1917) and *Aurelia, and Other Poems* (1920).

Sydney Oswald (1880–1926)
Pseudonym of Sydney Frederick McIllree Lomer, leading light of the Uranian circle. Friend of Edmund John and E. F. Benson. Professional soldier August 1899–July 1919, serving with 1st Battalion, Lancashire Fusiliers then 1st Battalion, King's Royal Rifle Corps. At outbreak of war Adjutant to 6th Battalion, Sherwood Foresters. Went to France in February 1915; invalided home with pneumonia in March 1915. Promoted from Captain to Major in September 1915. Attached to Egyptian Army March 1916–August 1917. Promoted to Temporary Lieutenant-Colonel in November 1917. Awarded OBE in 1919. War poems appear in anthology *Soldier Poets: Songs of the Fighting Men* (1916).

Wilfred Edward Salter Owen (1893–1918)
Born in Oswestry, and educated at Birkenhead Institute and Shrewsbury Technical School. Worked as a lay assistant to an Evangelical vicar at Dunsden 1911–1913, and as a language tutor in France 1913–1915. Returned to England and enlisted in Artists' Rifles in October 1915. Commissioned in June 1915 as a 2nd Lieutenant in 5th Battalion, Manchester

Regiment. Attached to 2nd Battalion in France in December 1915. Severely shell-shocked in May 1916 and invalided to Craiglockhart Hospital, Edinburgh in August, where he met Sassoon. Later met Graves, Osbert Sitwell, C. K. Scott Moncrieff and Philip Bainbrigge. Promoted to Lieutenant in December 1917. Returned to France in August 1918 and rejoined 2nd Battalion. Awarded MC in October and killed in action at the Sambre Canal on 4 November 1918. Editions of poems: *Poems* edited by Siegfried Sassoon (1920), *Poems* edited by Edmund Blunden (1931), *Collected Poems* edited by C. Day-Lewis (1963), *War Poems and Others* edited by Dominic Hibberd (1973) and *Complete Poems and Fragments* edited by Jon Stallworthy (1983).

Ezra Loomis Pound (1885–1972)
Born in Idaho, and educated at University of Pennsylvania and Hamilton College. Moved to Europe in 1908 and settled in London. Founded Imagism with Richard Aldington and Hilda Doolittle in 1912. Friend and champion of many writers, including T. S. Eliot, James Joyce and D. B. Wyndham Lewis. *Hugh Selwyn Mauberley* (1920) was being written as a comment on English life during the war. Left London in 1920 for Paris, and later moved to Rapallo, Italy. During the Second World War broadcast for Mussolini on Radio Rome and was subsequently charged with treason in 1945. Found unfit to plead, he was institutionalized from 1945–1961. Returned to Italy after release.

Frank Prewett (1893–1962)
Born in Ontario, and educated in Toronto and Christ Church, Oxford. Commissioned in November 1915 as a 2nd Lieutenant in Royal Field Artillery. Promoted to Lieutenant in July 1917. Served in France from 1916 and wounded in 1917. Met Sassoon, who christened him 'Toronto', at a convalescent hospital in London in December 1918. Also knew Graves. After the war became for a time a farmer in Oxfordshire. During Second World War served on a bomb-disposal squad in Birmingham and later undertook operational research for HQ Fighter Command and Supreme Command SEA. Worked for Air Ministry until 1954. War poems appear in *Poems* (1921) and *Collected Poems* (1964).

Herbert Edward Read (1893–1968)
Born at Kirbymoorside, Yorkshire, and educated at Crossley's School,

Halifax and Leeds University. Commissioned in January 1915 as a 2nd Lieutenant in 7th Battalion, Yorkshire Regiment. Served in France with 7th Battalion from November 1915–March 1916, 10th Battalion from April 1917–February 1918 and 2nd Battalion from February 1918. Promoted to Lieutenant in July 1917 and awarded Mention in Despatches, MC and DSO in 1918. After the war became distinguished art critic and eminent academic. Knighted in 1953. War experiences covered in *The Contrary Experience* (1963). War poems appear in *Naked Warriors* (1919) and *The End of a War* (1933).

Ernest Percival Rhys (1859–1946)
Born in Islington and educated in Bishop's Stortford, Hertfordshire and Newcastle-on-Tyne. Trained as a mining engineer but decided in 1886 to become a journalist in London. Member of Rhymer's Club in the 'Nineties and later editor of Everyman's Library. Friend of Ezra Pound, W. H. Davies, Louis Golding and Edward Thomas. War poems appear in *The Leaf Burners, and Other Poems* (1918) and *Rhymes for Everyone* (1933).

Edgell Rickword (1898–1982)
Joined Artists' Rifles from school in 1916. Commissioned in September 1917 as a 2nd Lieutenant in 5th Battalion, Royal Berkshire Regiment. Promoted to Lieutenant and awarded MC in March 1919. Invalided out after losing an eye. After the war became a noted literary critic, but after 1930 devoted himself to political journalism, editing the *Left Review* 1934–1938 and *Our Time* 1944–1947. Also wrote novels, short stories and verse. War poems appear in *Behind the Eyes* (1921) and *Invocation to Angels* (1928).

Owen Rutter (1899–1944) (Pseudonym 'Klip-klip')
Educated at St Paul's School. Worked as a District Commissioner in North Borneo. Commissioned in June 1915 as a 2nd Lieutenant in 7th Battalion, Wiltshire Regiment. Promoted to Lieutenant in April 1917 and to temporary Captain in May 1918. Served in France and Salonika 1915–1919. Demobilized in September 1919. War poem, *The Song of Tiadatha* (1919).

Siegfried Loraine Sassoon (1886–1967)
Born at Weirleigh, near Paddock Wood, Kent, and educated at Marlborough and Clare College, Cambridge. Enlisted in August 1914 as a Trooper in Sussex Yeomanry. Commissioned in May 1915 as a 2nd Lieutenant in 3rd

Battalion, Royal Welch Fusiliers and attached to 1st Battalion in November 1915 in France, where he met Robert Graves. Awarded MC in June 1916 and invalided home with trench fever in August 1916. Returned to France in February 1917 and joined 2nd Battalion, Royal Welch Fusiliers. Wounded in shoulder in April 1917 and invalided home. Publicly protested against the war in June 1917 and sent to Craiglockhart Hospital in Edinburgh, where he met Wilfred Owen. Promoted to Lieutenant in July 1917 and passed for active service in November 1917. Posted to Ireland in January 1918, then attached to 25th Battalion, Royal Welch Fusiliers in Palestine in February 1918. Battalion moved to France in May 1918. Received head wound in July 1918 and invalided home. Demobilized with rank of Captain in March 1919. War experiences covered in the novels *Memoirs of a Fox-hunting Man* (1928), *Memoirs of an Infantry Officer* (1930), *Sherston's Progress* (1936), the autobiography *Siegfried's Journey* (1945), and *Siegfried Sassoon Diaries 1915–1918* (1983). War poems appear in *The Old Huntsman, and Other Poems* (1917), *Counter-Attack, and Other Poems* (1918), *Picture Show* (1919), *War Poems* (1919), *The Heart's Journey* (1920) and *The War Poems* (1983).

Edward Richard Buxton Shanks (1892–1965)
Born in London, and educated at Merchant Taylor's School and Trinity College, Cambridge. Editor of *Granta* 1912–1913. Enlisted in Artists' Rifles in August 1914 and commissioned in December 1914 as a 2nd Lieutenant in 8th Battalion, South Lancashire Regiment. Invalided out of the service in April 1915 before serving abroad. Worked at the War Office until 1918. After the war became one of the leading Georgians, and a prolific novelist, biographer and essayist. First winner of Hawthornden Prize in 1919, assistant editor of *London Mercury* 1919–1922, Lecturer in Poetry, Liverpool University 1926 and chief leader-writer for the *Evening Standard* 1928–1935. War poems appear in *Poems* (1916) and *The Queen of China, and Other Poems* (1919).

Henry Lamont Simpson (1897–1918)
Born in Carlisle, and educated at Carlisle Grammar School and Pembroke College, Cambridge. Commissioned in June 1917 as a 2nd Lieutenant in 1st Battalion, Lancashire Fusiliers and went to France in August 1917. Became battalion intelligence officer and was killed on patrol at Hazebrouck on 29 August 1918. War poems appear in *Moods and Tenses* (1919).

Philip Edward Thomas (1878–1917)
Born in London, and educated at St Paul's School and Lincoln College, Cambridge. Before the war worked as as essayist and reviewer. Friend of Brooke, Gibson, W. H. Davies and other Georgians. Encouraged to write poetry by American poet Robert Frost. Enlisted in July 1915 in Artists' Rifles and commissioned as a 2nd Lieutenant in 244th Siege Battery, Royal Garrison Artillery in August 1916. Went to France in January 1917 and killed in action at Arras on 9 April 1917. All his poetry was written between November 1914 and January 1917 before his departure for France. Editions of poems: *Poems* (1917), *Last Poems* (1918) and *Collected Poems* (1978).

W. G. Thomas
Educated at Exeter College, Oxford and worked as a master at Queen Mary's Grammar School, Walsall. Commissioned in August 1914 as a 2nd Lieutenant in 90th Winnipeg Rifles. Transferred to 9th Battalion, Royal Welch Fusiliers in February 1915 and promoted to Lieutenant. Went to France in July 1915 and awarded MC in January 1916. Promoted to Captain in March 1916. Instructor at Lewis Gun Schools from April 1917 and transferred to Machine Gun Corps in July 1917. Demobilized in March 1919. War poems appear in *The Song of the Lewis Gun* (1917) (with A. S. Barnard) and *Amateur Soldiers* (1928).

A 'Tommy'
Presumably served in France. Author of *If I Goes West!* (1918).

Eric Fitzwater Wilkinson (1891–1917)
Born in Portesham, near Weymouth, Dorset, and educated at Grammar Schools of Dorchester and Ilkley and University of Leeds. Became master at Ilkley Grammar School in 1911 and member of OTC. Commissioned in October 1914 as a 2nd Lieutenant in 6th Battalion, West Yorkshire Regiment. Transferred to 1/8th Battalion and went to France in April 1915. Awarded MC in July 1915 at St Julien, and two Mention in Despatches. Promoted to Lieutenant in August 1915 and to Captain in June 1916. Gassed at Nieuport in July 1917 and invalided home. Returned to France in September 1917 and killed in action at Passchendaele Ridge on 9 October 1917. War poems appear in *Sunrise Dreams, and Other Poems* (1916).

George Willis
Served in the ranks in France. War poems appear in *Any Soldier to his Son* (1919) and *A Ballad of Four Brothers* (1921).

Fabian Strachey Woodley (1888–1957)
Born in Taunton, Somerset, and educated at Cheltenham College and University College, Oxford. Commissioned in September 1914 as a 2nd Lieutenant in 8th Battalion, Royal Munster Fusiliers. Went to France in December 1915 and wounded in September 1916. Promoted to Lieutenant in October 1916 and awarded MC in November 1916. Transferred to 1st Battalion in May 1917 and from December 1917–October 1918 attached to 8th and 2nd Battalions, Royal Irish Rifles. Promoted to Acting Captain in September 1918 and demobilized in October 1919. After the war worked for *Somerset Local Gazette*. Moved into teaching and became an English master at several schools including Wellington. Friend of artist Henry Scott Tuke. Mentioned in *Love in Earnest*. War poems appear in *A Crown of Friendship, and Other Poems* (1921).

James Stanley Yates (189 –1915)
Born in Claygate, near Esher, Surrey, and educated at King's School, Canterbury and Hertford College, Oxford. Master at St Bees School and member of OTC from December 1912. Commissioned in April 1915 as a 2nd Lieutenant in 3rd Battalion, Royal West Kent Regiment. Went to France with 6th Battalion in June 1915 and killed in action at Loos on 8 October 1915. War poems appear in *War Lyrics, and Other Poems* (1919).

Edward Hilton Young (1879–1960)
Educated at Eton and Trinity College, Oxford. Commissioned in August 1914 as a Lieutenant in Royal Naval Volunteer Reserve. Awarded DSC for bringing naval guns ashore at Nieuport les Bains in 1915, Bar to DSC for blocking of Zeebrugge in 1918, and DSO for service on the Archangel Front against the Bolsheviks in 1919. Promoted to Lieutenant-Commander in April 1918. Member of Parliament 1915–1935, with various ministerial appointments including Minister of Health 1931–1935. Became Lord Kennet in 1935. Active on many commissions and delegate to League of Nations. War experiences covered in *By Land and Sea* (1920). War poems appear in *The Muse at Sea* (1919).

BIBLIOGRAPHY

ELLIS, JOHN, *Eye-deep in Hell*, Croom Helm, 1976

FUSSELL, PAUL, *The Great War and Modern Memory*, OUP, 1975

HIBBERD, DOMINIC, *Owen the Poet*, Macmillan, 1987

PARKER, PETER, *The Old Lie: the Great War and the Public School Ethos*, Constable, 1987

READE, BRIAN, *Sexual Heretics*, Routledge & Kegan Paul, 1970

RUTHERFORD, ANDREW, *The Literature of War: Five Studies in Heroic Virtue*, Macmillan, 1978

SMITH, TIMOTHY D'ARCH, *Love in Earnest: Some Notes on the Lives and Writings of 'Uranian' Poets from 1889–1930*, Routledge & Kegan Paul, 1970

SMITH, MALVERN VAN WYCK, *Drummer Hodge: The Poetry of the Anglo-Boer War (1899–1902)*, OUP, 1978

SPEAR, HILDA D., *Remembering we Forget: A Background Study to the Poetry of the First World War*, Davis-Poynter, 1979

INDEX